A WORKING MODEL FOR CONTINGENT FACULTY

Precarity & Contingency
Series Editors: Sue Doe and Seth Kahn

The Precarity & Contingency book series publishes scholarship—broadly construed to include empirical (both quantitative and qualitative), historical, and critical/theoretical projects—that addresses precarious academic labor. While its focus is primarily on academic labor in higher education, it encourages projects that address other labor issues on campuses (including K-12) and/or precarity in labor sectors outside education. The series embraces new visions of and innovations in leadership in the academic environment that might more effectively address current labor crises. It also encourages projects that explore intersections of academic labor activism with other forms of activism, such as LGBTQ+, gender, race equality, ability/disability activism, and environmentalism, among others.

The WAC Clearinghouse, University Press of Colorado, and the Colorado State University Center for the Study of Academic Labor are collaborating so that these books will be widely available through free digital distribution and low-cost print editions. The publishers and the series editors are committed to the principle that knowledge should freely circulate and have embraced the use of technology to support open access to scholarly work.

A WORKING MODEL FOR CONTINGENT FACULTY

By Robert Samuels

The WAC Clearinghouse
wac.colostate.edu
Fort Collins, Colorado

University Press of Colorado
upcolorado.com
Denver, Colorado

The WAC Clearinghouse, Fort Collins, Colorado 80523

University Press of Colorado, Denver, Colorado 80202

ISBN 978-1-64215-176-3 (PDF) | 978-1-64215-177-0 (ePub) | 978-1-64642-396-5 (pbk.)

DOI 10.37514/PRC-B.2023.1763

Produced in the United States of America

Library of Congress Cataloging-in-Publication Data

Names: Samuels, Robert, 1961– author.
Title: A working model for contingent faculty / by Robert Samuels.
Description: Fort Collins, Colorado : The WAC Clearinghouse ; Denver, Colorado : University Press of Colorado, [2023] | Series: Precarity & contingency | Includes bibliographical references.
Identifiers: LCCN 2023000314 (print) | LCCN 2023000315 (ebook) | ISBN 9781646423965 (Paperback) | ISBN 9781642151763 (Adobe pdf) | ISBN 9781642151770 (epub)
Subjects: LCSH: College teachers, Part-time–United States. | College teachers, Part-time–Salaries, etc.–United States. | College teachers–Tenure–United States. | Universities and colleges–Faculty. | Education, Higher–United States.
Classification: LCC LB2331.72 .S34 2023 (print) | LCC LB2331.72 (ebook) | DDC 378.1/20973–dc23/ eng/20230126
LC record available at https://lccn.loc.gov/2023000314
LC ebook record available at https://lccn.loc.gov/2023000315

Copyeditor: Karen Peirce
Designer: Mike Palmquist
Cover Art: "Force Forge II, Chattanooga, Tennessee," by Malcolm Childers. Used with permission.
Series Editors: Sue Doe and Seth Kahn

The WAC Clearinghouse supports teachers of writing across the disciplines. Hosted by Colorado State University, it brings together scholarly journals and book series as well as resources for teachers who use writing in their courses. This book is available in digital formats for free download at wac.colostate.edu.

Founded in 1965, the University Press of Colorado is a nonprofit cooperative publishing enterprise supported, in part, by Adams State University, Colorado State University, Fort Lewis College, Metropolitan State University of Denver, University of Alaska Fairbanks, University of Colorado, University of Denver, University of Northern Colorado, University of Wyoming, Utah State University, and Western Colorado University. For more information, visit upcolorado.com.

Land Acknowledgment. The Colorado State University Land Acknowledgment can be found at https://landacknowledgment.colostate.edu.

Contents

P&C

A WORKING MODEL FOR CONTINGENT FACULTY

Chapter 1. Introduction

This book outlines what fair and effective practices for contingent faculty can look like. Drawing from more than 20 years of union activism and university teaching, I examine programs, policies, and practices that work for non-tenure-track (NTT) faculty. This detailed analysis of facts on the ground will be one of the first of its kind, and I hope that it will help contingent faculty members fight for better working conditions. Throughout this book, I focus on issues concerning academic freedom, job security, compensation, shared governance, promotion, evaluation, benefits, and dispute resolution for NTT faculty.

The intended audience for this work is not only NTT faculty members and union and non-union organizers, but I also hope to interest people concerned about higher education in general and about the broader labor market. Since so many jobs now are low wage and part time, it is vital to see how working conditions can be improved for all precarious laborers.

Although much of this book was written before the COVID-19 pandemic, the basic arguments and analysis are still relevant and valid. What the current crisis has changed is the intensification of certain trends rendering precarious faculty even more precarious (Tam and Jacoby n.p.). Not only are more contingent faculty seeing their job security and compensation reduced, but universities and colleges have also eliminated many tenure-track (TT) jobs (Shillington et al. 501). Moreover, the move to remote learning has increased the potential for administrative power as it has enhanced the possibility of surveillance of the faculty (Day et al. 4). Due to the need for social distancing and the reduction of in-person education, the organizing of precarious faculty members has also been harmed (Fay and Ghadimi 815). However, what has not changed is the need to improve the working conditions of contingent instructors in higher education. The model presented in this book is not only more fair and more just than many of the existing higher education employment structures, but it is also achievable through sustained collective organizing.

A Short History of Contingent Faculty

Much of my knowledge on this topic comes from my experience being a lecturer at the University of California, Santa Barbara (UCSB) and the University of California, Los Angeles (UCLA) and my 13 years as union president representing contingent faculty in the University of California (UC) system. Although many of my examples will come from the UC system, following the lead of Heidi McGrew and Joe Untener, I draw on my local experience to define good practices that can be used in different types of institutions. One of my concerns motivating this work is that when we concentrate on bad practices, we can become depressed and de-mobilized, so it is essential to look at what has been done and

P&C

what can be done in the future to improve the working conditions of contingent faculty members.

Throughout this book, I define precarious faculty members as people who are not eligible for tenure. At times, I use the term contingent, while at other times, I use the term precarious. While many graduate student instructors also fall into the category of precarious, I focus mainly on part-time and full-time non-tenure-track instructors who are not graduate students. The reason for this definition of contingency is that I believe, like Adrianna Kezar and Cecile Sam, that a major distinction must be made between those who do and do not have the possibility of gaining the job security that goes along with tenure ("Governance as a Catalyst" n.p.).

Much of this book is concerned with the ways contingent faculty are perceived by other people within higher education institutions and how these faculty members perceive themselves. I seek to explain the causes for the situation in which contingent faculty, who make up the majority of faculty members, do not share the same basic rights and treatment as their more privileged TT colleagues (White n.p.). As I argued in *Educating Inequality*, higher education not only tends to enhance economic inequality but also socializes students to see inequality as inevitable (Samuels 4–6). What is interesting is that not only does college on average increase social and economic inequality for students, but also it tends to do the same thing to the faculty by producing and rationalizing an academic hierarchy.

● The Cause of Contingency

Many people have argued about the causes for this hierarchy in higher education (Pratt 264; Thompson, "Alchemy in the Academy" 278; Brill; Gulli 1), and while this book focuses more on the solutions to the problem, I do want to begin by offering an explanation for the creation and maintenance of academic precarity. The most convincing narrative I have encountered is derived from Robert Nisbet's book *The Degradation of the Academic Dogma*. Nisbet argues that after World War II, governmental funding for scientific research and Cold War defense made its way to American research universities. This new source of revenue radically restructured these institutions as many science faculty realized that they could make more money and receive more prestige if they focused on externally funded research. One problem that arose was who would teach the undergraduate students. At first, universities turned to graduate students, but eventually they started to hire a growing number of NTT teaching-centered faculty.

This situation created an academic social hierarchy that still structures higher education today with research valued over teaching, the sciences privileged over the humanities, graduate education prioritized over undergraduate instruction, theory promoted over practice, faculty emphasized over students, and prestige favored over the public mission (Samuels, *Educating Inequality* 121). Within research universities, these structural hierarchies also rationalize an economic and political hierarchy so that researchers are compensated at a higher rate than teachers. In the case of introductory courses, such as those in composition, languages, and math, the main focus on teaching undergraduate students how to improve a particular skill places these instructors on the lower end of all of the class hierarchies. In other words, in order to justify paying certain faculty less money, a set of institutional hierarchies and prejudices have to be activated and maintained.

● Generating Prestige

One of the key lessons we can gather from Nisbet's historical narrative is the idea that the exploitation of contingent academic labor is not primarily the result of evil administrators or budget-cutting state politicians; rather, professors responding to incentives were driven to outsource the non-lucrative and non-prestige-generating aspects of their jobs. Moreover, this internal dynamic fed into a central tenant of Marx's economic theory, which is that the more valuable a job is for society, the less it will be compensated because people do not want to pay for necessary things like childcare, cleaning, and other tasks that have been traditionally labeled as female labor (Lebowitz 16–36).

It is vital to stress that labor hierarchies are shaped by cultural prejudices, and these forms of discrimination serve to justify and naturalize the exploitation of workers. The inverse of this system of extracting surplus value from debased members of the social hierarchy is the generation of a prestige economy based on the scarcity of a valued object (Blackmore and Kandiko 403–411). For instance, I was once at a meeting at UCLA where the criteria for tenure and whether two books should be the new benchmark was being discussed. A senior professor got up and said, "When you open a rare book, it loses half of its value. Our faculty should write books that no one ever opens." This story points to the underlying irrational logic of the prestige economy (Daly 67). Value is often defined by its non-use value, while something that is very useful has to be devalued (Eaton and Eswaran 1088-104).

● Cynical Conformity

To comprehend how contingent faculty are affected by these academic structures, we have to see the ways the dominant form of subjectivity in higher education is cynical conformity (Sloterdijk n.p.). For example, schools will say that rankings of them do not measure anything of real value, but the same schools try to compete to raise their status. In this case, cynical conformity means that people aim to succeed in a system in which they do not believe. This same logic applies to the use of student evaluations to assess the quality of teaching. Most institutions now know that these tools are not scientific and that they are highly biased, but they are still being used (Merritt 235–38). Cynical conformity also helps to explain the use of large lecture classes, grades, and biased admissions standards. In other words, virtually everything going on in higher education is mediated by the attitude of conformity from a distance (Žižek and Laclau 104).

If we use Peter Sloterdijk's theory of cynical conformity to think about the treatment of contingent faculty, we realize that even though many people know that the system of relying on contingent faculty is ethically wrong, it is still used because people are simply conforming to a structure in which they do not believe. The question then is how do we change this culture and counter cynical conformity? My experience is that a central tool for promoting positive social change is giving people something in which they believe. For contingent faculty, this may mean starting first with the attitude that their work is essential and should not be the target of prejudice and discrimination. It also means moving second to the idea that these teachers need to join together to fight for better working conditions, which can be done by forming a union or another type of collective organization.

As illustrated by Georgette Fleischer's "Come Together, Right Now/Over Me, Over You, Over Us," many people within the contingent faculty movement believe the best way to fight for better working conditions is to shame administrators and professors by revealing the unjust nature of the exploitation of precarious teachers. My experience has been that this appeal to justice rarely works and what is needed is collective power in order to counter institutional power. Since contingent teachers now make up the majority of the faculty, they should be able to organize themselves to demand better treatment, but this requires forming group solidarity fueled by a vision of a better future (Kezar, "Needed Policies" 2).

What I hope to present in this work is a view of the ways different groups have been able to improve the working lives of contingent faculty in the United States. By providing concrete examples of specific practices and policies, I present models that all contingent faculty can seek to attain. Although I do not think that one model fits all situations, it is important to look at actual ways contingent faculty have improved their working conditions (Doe and Palmquist 23). Part of this work requires understanding the diversity of precarious academic positions while outlining the way change can happen at higher education institutions. In using the example of other minority rights social movements, I examine the relation between campaigns for social justice and the desire to attain fair and equitable treatment both inside and outside of the academy.

● Book Outline

Chapter 2 describes the content and effects of the union contract representing over 6,500 contingent faculty in the UC system. One of my main goals in this section is to present best practices that can be developed both inside and outside of a unionized institution. Not only do I provide information on effective review and promotion policies for NTT faculty, but also I discuss how to integrate teaching, research, and service into the assessable workload for instructors who are not eligible for tenure. A key idea presented in this chapter is the need to base contracts and working conditions on shared principles.

In Chapter 3, I examine different ways contingent faculty can organize to improve their working conditions. I discuss here the structure and logic of progressive social movements and specific methods precarious contingent workers have used to make their workplaces more democratic. My overall goal is to provide examples of what is possible if precarious faculty work together to improve their jobs.

The fourth chapter analyses the ways the actual practices I describe go against many of the myths and prejudices concerning precarious faculty. In looking closely at Herb Childress' book *The Adjunct Underclass*, I reveal how even a sympathetic portrayal of contingent faculty can recirculate destructive stereotypes and blind us from seeing more progressive possibilities. While I do not want to minimize the negative working conditions facing most precarious academic labor, I feel it is important to balance the representation of negative aspects with positive possibilities. After all, why should people fight for improvements if they do not think it is possible to make progressive changes?

Chapter 5 examines Michael Bérubé and Jennifer Ruth's exploration, in *The Humanities, Higher Education, and Academic Freedom*, of providing tenure to contingent faculty members. Although these well-intentioned professors seek to help the cause of NTT faculty, their work actually exposes many of the destructive prejudices that tenured allies often hold in relation to contingent faculty members. To counter some of these prejudices and to offer a different vision of the future, I argue that full-time, non-tenure-track (FTNTT) positions offer an alternative to the binary opposition between tenure and pure contingency.

Chapter 6 concludes the book by focusing on the role of contingent faculty in the new "gig academy" as defined by Adrianna Kezar and colleagues in their book *The Gig Academy*. In looking at the changing nature of work in higher education and in the general economy, I offer ways of rethinking workplace democracy. One of my central arguments is that those of us with experience in improving the working conditions of contingent faculty in higher education can use that experience to improve the lives of millions of workers in the general economy who are now being misclassified as contract laborers.

Chapter 2. Effective Practices and Policies for Contingent Faculty

The main goal of this chapter is to document actual practices affecting contingent faculty in the UC system and at other colleges and universities in order to provide examples for people striving to improve the working conditions of precarious academic workers. In looking at current policies concerning compensation, benefits, workload, job security, promotion, academic freedom, and other vital areas of academic life, I present concrete models for making these jobs more fair and effective on both an educational and organizational level. It is important to point out that I do not claim that the labor conditions for contingent faculty in the UC system are ideal, but I do believe that collective action has led to some very positive, progressive changes. I also want to stress that most of the practices I discuss can be achieved without unionization, and many of these contractual obligations have migrated to non-unionized worksites (Dobbie and Robinson 132).

On the most basic level, fair and just working conditions provide for employees a sense that they are a valued part of a community and that they have the opportunity to pursue a sustainable career in terms of compensation and benefits. It also means that they are given the resources to do one's job in an effective manner and that they are provided with a clear and objective system to evaluate their work. According to this universalistic logic, everyone should be judged in an unbiased and transparent manner. Of course, these goals of objectivity, transparency, and universality are impossible ideals to fully achieve, and yet modern democracy and science are shaped by the pursuit of these goals. In a spirit of pragmatic idealism, this book seeks to detail different ways to make the conditions of precarious employment more just and fair while still recognizing the limitations inherent in these positions.

● The UC System

Since it is the structure and reality I know best, I will begin by examining the ten campus UC system where only the NTT faculty are unionized, while the faculty who are eligible for tenure do not have a collective bargaining agreement (Tingle). Moreover, both part-time and full-time NTT faculty are covered by the same compensation structure and have all of the same rights and benefits, except that healthcare and retirement support only starts when someone works at least half time. By not distinguishing between part-time and full-time positions, the shared contract regulating over 6,500 UC faculty has allowed for a wide variety of employment situations.[1] Since there are many NTT professionals who want

---

1. For research on the various types of working conditions for precarious academic labor, see Feldman and Turnley; Monks; Palmquist et al.; and Kezar and Maxey, "Troubling Ethical Lapses."

to teach only one course a year while others want to be full-time lecturers, it was necessary to develop a contract that could cover all of these different situations. The solution was to base everything on the percentage of one's appointment; for example, if the minimum starting salary for all lecturers is $52,000, and one teaches half of a full load, one is paid $26,000.

With this model, because most people do not know what percentage appointment other people have, there is often less of an obvious hierarchy in the workplace in which everyone is supposed to be treated by the same basic rules and practices. For instance, all of the lecturers come up for a major review in their sixth year regardless of the percentage of their appointment, and the results of that review can lead to a continuing appointment. Once someone has a continuing appointment, they can be let go only for very specific reasons, and this has rarely happened. All continuing appointments are also reviewed every three years for a merit increase, and the minimum for these increases (currently six percent of one's salary) has been negotiated for everyone (Fichtenbaum). There are also cost of living increases that once again are given to all faculty regardless of the percentage of their appointment. The first lesson, then, for anyone pursuing better working conditions for contingent faculty is to push for more equality. However, at the same time, contracts and polices have to remain flexible in order to account for the different types of employment some workers prefer or that are necessary because of institutional needs. While it is important to limit the push for maximum administrative flexibility, it is also vital to recognize the need for employees to have varied and flexible employment opportunities. There is thus a necessary dialectical relationship between universal rules and particular labor conditions.

In many ways, the NTT positions in the UC system offer a middle ground between traditional TT professorships and many current, contingent positions.[2] Furthermore, even though most lecturers are hired primarily to be teachers, usually they are also required to do service and participate in professional development. In this structure, administrators cannot say that lecturers only teach, so it is harder to rationalize paying them less or not respecting them. The shared union contract also creates a more standardized system of treatment and compensation; although there is also plenty of freedom for individual departments to reward people at a higher rate or to come up with their own polices as long as they do not conflict with the collective bargaining agreement.[3] Once again, a key concept is to have clear rules and policies that allow for a certain level of flexibility but do not give the administration free hand at controlling the terms and conditions of the employment situation, and by management, I am referring to anyone who can make a decision to rehire or not rehire an employee.

---

2. For research on full-time, non-tenure-track positions, see Levin and Shaker.

3. Collective bargaining agreements for non-tenure-track faculty are examined in Rhoades, "Bargaining Quality"; Kezar and Maxey, "Missing from the Institutional Data Picture"; and Rhoades and Maitland.

● Professional Development

Since many lecturers are reviewed based on their teaching, service, and professional development, the UC-AFT union fought to have a special funding source to support grants for travel to conferences or for help paying for research projects. Once again, an emphasis is placed on the fact that many of these faculty members do very different things, so they should be rewarded for what they do rather than devalued for what they do not do. The union also fights hard to make sure that all review processes are fair and transparent and that there is a way to challenge unfair reviews, even though in the current contract, only the process of the review can be grieved and not the actual academic judgment. This review process stands in contrast to what happens at other universities and colleges where NTT instructors are routinely fired based on student evaluations of teaching (Heller A8). Of course, in order for any system to work, there has to be a process of accountability and enforcement; otherwise, effective processes and policies will be vulnerable to being ignored or transgressed (Kahn A14). In fact, when I have consulted with other unions about their contracts, I always first look at the enforcement mechanisms to see if the contract provisions can be policed. The lesson here is that it is not good enough to achieve better practices if those practices can be easily violated.

It is important to stress that many of the practices I am outlining here can be implemented at non-unionized institutions, but the problem remains of how to make sure these policies are followed and protected. For instance, a university in a right-to-work state may create a professional development fund for contingent faculty, yet in times of economic hardship or shifting priorities, the institutions may abandon this source of support. In contrast, when a professional development fund is mandated by a collective bargaining agreement, it is harder for this policy to be reversed or undermined. Still, it is vital for non-unionized faculty to fight for this type of support even if it cannot be fully protected. In other words, it is usually best to have a union, but in the case where one does not exist, employees can still strive to replicate many aspects of a collective bargaining agreement. For instance, a non-unionized group of contingent faculty can document who promised support that was removed or reduced. By documenting policies in a transparent way, it becomes harder for these new achievements to be removed when a new administrator arrives.

The category of professional development has played a key role in allowing many UC contingent faculty to be reviewed and rewarded for a wide variety of activities. For some lecturers, professional development means going to conferences; for others, it entails developing a new course or publishing a scholarly article. The inclusion of professional development in the contract has proven essential because it prevents administrators from arguing that NTT faculty "only" teach. At the same time, the contract's broad definition of professional development recognizes that there are many different types of precarious academic labor and many different motivations for people holding these positions.

When members have been surveyed, results have showed that some are professionals with full-time jobs outside of the university, while others are part-time workers who would like to teach more classes. There are also many full-time lecturers who end up taking TT jobs at other institutions, and some faculty ask to have their appointments reduced in order to tend to family matters or for other professional activities.

● Recognizing Work

One of the more challenging aspects of the contract between UC and the American Federation of Teachers (AFT) has been the question of workload. While the contract states that the maximum number of courses assigned to any one instructor over three quarters should be nine, many departments have lower levels, and there are several ways for faculty to qualify for a course replacement.[4] Faculty can get a course reduction for serving on committees, teaching large classes, advising students, and a whole host of other activities that often go uncompensated. The guiding principle behind this part of the contract is that contingent faculty should be recognized and rewarded for all of the different academic activities they perform.[5] However, this part of the contract has been difficult to fully enforce, and it requires constant monitoring.

The contract also states that NTT faculty should have their full academic freedom rights protected. This stands in contrast to the situation at many other institutions (Marshall, 46–48). Since NTT faculty in the UC system have the same protections as tenured professors, they are able to bring up any dispute in the academic senate or through the union dispute resolution process. Yet, even with the same rights as tenured professors, contingent faculty often have their academic freedom threatened by the use of student evaluations (Samuels, "Contingent Faculty" A23). Since many departments rely heavily on these evaluations to promote and reward NTT faculty, these instructors may have to teach in a defensive manner so that they do not offend or upset their students. While the union has negotiated a reduction to the reliance on these evaluations for reviews, it has been unable to convince the university to completely eliminate the use of student evaluations or reduce their influence even more. What it has been able to do is to push for a process of evaluating faculty in their sixth year, and this includes recommending that the faculty have their classes visited by fellow lecturers and that lecturers serve on the review committees. This recommendation is in line with best practices (Kezar and Sam, "Institutionalizing Equitable Policies"; Heller A10-A11). It should be clear that for any union or non-union group seeking to improve the working conditions

---

4. Workload for contingent faculty is discussed in Rhoades and Maitland; and Kezar and Sam, "Understanding the New Majority."

5. The UC-AFT contract is available at https://ucnet.universityofcalifornia.edu /labor/bargaining-units/ix/contract.html.

of their members, establishing clear and fair methods for hiring, rehiring, and promotion is essential.

Another important area of best practices and policies for contingent academic labor involves making sure that these faculty members have the proper material conditions to do their work. This includes office space, access to computers, proper administrative support, and other needed resources (Fels et al. A15). While working conditions still vary widely in the UC system, there has been an effort to make sure that all are given the opportunity to do their jobs in an effective manner, and this at times requires using the grievance process to force departments to provide the proper resources. The UC system's complicated dispute resolution process begins with steps at the local level, but if the department or the dean cannot resolve the problem to the mutual satisfaction of both sides, it moves to an outside court arbitrator. Since the university usually does not want to risk being overruled or having to face large legal fees, it often resolves things before they get to arbitration.

The union has also pushed to make sure that lecturers are always recognized for the work that they are doing, which includes getting programs to list the names of lecturers on course schedules and departmental web sites. Moreover, the union has spent a great deal of effort ensuring that all faculty have the proper job title so that the university does not try to replace protected lecturers with other unprotected faculty, such as visiting professors who are actually visiting from nowhere. Since universities are constantly coming up with new job titles that often function to remove workers from protected groups, it is important to constantly police these new positions (Kezar and Maxey, "Missing from the Institutional Data Picture").

● Guiding Principles

Even in institutions that are not unionized, there are many examples of places where precarious academic labor has organized collectively to protect their working conditions (Kezar, "Preface" xv–xvi; Street et al.; Goldstene, 7). However, the first step is to see what is possible and what has worked and not worked in the past. My hope is that outlining the working conditions of contingent faculty can help to provide information and inspiration for all faculty seeking to improve their employment situations. Although I do not think that one size fits all or that we have found the perfect solution to many of the problems facing precarious academic labor, I do believe we have made some important progress in these areas.

One of the guiding principles behind the UC-AFT contract and collective organizing is the idea that the work done by contingent faculty is as important as anyone else's in the university system. In fact, some lecturers feel that they are the protectors of undergraduate education, making their labor the most vital (Morris). In this context, the relationship between tenured and non-tenured faculty varies greatly, but for the most part, there is a general level of benign indifference. I believe the reason for this situation at the UC system is that the majority of the faculty and administrators now recognize that it takes many different types of employees to make a university effective, so one has to recognize and respect the need for everyone to be able to do their job in an effective manner. As I will show in later chapters, this acknowledgment of the diversity of employment situations is often lacking elsewhere; instead, people rely on stereotypes, prejudices, and over-generalization in their perceptions of contingent academic labor. To counter these destructive representations, it is essential to offer alternative perspectives and practices.

● Existing Problems in the UC Model

Although the existing model for contingent faculty in the UC system does provide many examples of better working conditions for precarious academic labor, there are still many areas that need to be improved. One particular problem is the way that student evaluations are used to assess the quality of a contingent faculty member's teaching. The union has tried to eliminate this biased system of evaluation, but the university administration has argued that no one wants to spend the time and money on a more effective system. It is simply cheaper and faster to have students make a judgment regarding the quality of their learning environments. Even when the union points out that these evaluations are not scientific and that they are often influenced by racism and sexism (Huston 598–600), the university system resists any alternative. Fortunately, there is a growing movement to provide models for more effective assessment practices, such as the example Jeffrey L. Buller provides with his book *Best Practices in Faculty Evaluation*, and the threat of lawsuits against the biased nature of these instruments may force a change. What has been achieved in the UC system is language stating that the numerical part of the student evaluations cannot be the sole criteria in assessing lecturers, and a list of other methods that should be employed, including class observations, self-assessments, and course materials, has been provided. Still, many departments simply refuse to review their lecturers until they get to their major sixth-year review, and this lack of a required review process has contributed to a high level of turnover for people in their first few years.

Another continuing issue is that since contingent faculty have few job protections before they earn a continuing appointment, some departments have tried to prevent teachers from getting to their sixth-year review by only hiring them for a few years. Contractual language has been negotiated that prevents programs from simply getting rid of people to prevent them from reaching their sixth-year review, but this part of the contract has been very hard to enforce. Still, for any faculty group seeking to enhance job protections, it is necessary to find ways to protect precarious academic labor against the administrative desire to maximize flexibility and cut costs by refusing to let experienced teachers gain job security. One way of enhancing job protections is to clearly spell out under what conditions a person can be hired or not hired (Maitland and Rhoades 78–80); for instance, it can be required that each time someone is not brought back to teach, an official reason has to be given in writing to the union and the affected person. In the UC system, once a department is forced to come up with an explanation in written form, it seems to be more likely to think twice about what it is doing. Another strategy is to require extended notification for any type of layoff or reduction in time (Maitland and Rhoades 78). Once again, even if contingent faculty members do not have collective bargaining rights, they can band together and create a collective organization that negotiates better working conditions or pushes the faculty senate to enact better policies and procedures.

In the UC system, some departments do have fair employment process, but other programs, even at the same institution, do not treat their contingent faculty in the same way. Often the reason why one department is better than the other is because one program has a critical mass of NTT faculty. When there are only a few contingent instructors in a program, it is easier for them to be exploited or even let go for no clear reason. A way of overcoming this problem is to share information about best practices to make sure that faculty from different departments communicate with each other. Such communication across departments can be achieved through joint meetings, online newsletters, and door-to-door canvassing.

Within the UC system, some departments simply ignore the contract because they do not know what is in it and because their faculty have not been informed about their rights. Luckily, a new state law has required all institutions to have orientations for new union members, but even in non-unionized workplaces, it is vital to provide all new employees with a clear understanding of their rights and responsibilities. Unfortunately, many faculty members only find out about their rights when they are violated, and it is by then often too late to do anything about the issue. As I will discuss in the next chapter, a key to preventing this from happening is to develop a network of organizers who talk to faculty in different departments on a regular basis.

● Other Models and Institutions

To present some of the ways different institutions have produced a wide-range of policies and practices for contingent faculty, I will now turn to one positive model found at Vancouver Community College (VCC) and profiled by Kezar and Daniel Maxey in *The Changing Faculty and Student Success*:

> Faculty at VCC are classified as either 'regular', which is the functional equivalent of tenure, or 'term' employees. Virtually all faculty have the opportunity for job security. There is one hiring process and after at least two years of at least 50% full-time employment all term faculty are automatically converted to regular status. (1)

For community colleges without a research mission, this model helps to fight against faculty turnover and creates a fair and transparent career path. Moreover, at VCC, when courses become available, the "part-time faculty have the right of first refusal," and once they teach these courses for two years, their "employment status is increased accordingly" (1). In this structure, all of the faculty are compensated according to "a standardized pay scale," and like the UC system, part-time faculty who achieve "50% full-time employment have access to almost all the same benefits as regular faculty including healthcare, dental, paid vacation, and professional development funds and leave time" (1). In this text, Kezar and Maxey further point out that all faculty at VCC are also given full rights to participate in their departmental and institution-wide governance (1).

A different model for protecting contingent faculty can be found in the Pennsylvania State System of Higher Education, where, as William B. Lalicker and Amy Lynch-Biniek explain, FTNTT faculty can be converted to TT positions after five years of service by a vote of the majority of the faculty (91–92). Lalicker and Lynch-Biniek note that this system of conversion has not resolved all labor problems (91), but it does offer a new model for increased job security, which will be discussed in the next chapter.

In addition, some institutions, such as Clackamas Community College, Mount San Antonio College, San Francisco State University, and the University of Southern California, are starting to include all faculty in their shared governance (Kezar and Maxey, *Changing Faculty* 3), and this has resulted in better awareness of the pay and workload challenges for contingent faculty. The idea here is that one of the best ways to make contingent jobs more fair and equitable is to give these employees more democratic rights.

While there are many examples of different institutions improving the working conditions of contingent faculty, it is hard to tell what is really happening unless one is on the ground and can see how particular policies are actually enacted. One reason why I have focused primarily on my own institution in this chapter is because I have first-hand knowledge of how the contract is enacted on a daily basis and how the different parts of the contract fit together. As I have stressed throughout this chapter, a key thing to consider when attempting to increase the job security of contingent faculty is the enforcement mechanisms for particular policies. For instance, if one provides increased security after six years, what prevents an institution from simply removing people in their first six years? Moreover, if a school requires NTT faculty to do service and research in order to be promoted, how does the university or college financially support these activities? One of the most effective defenses against the practice of removing contingent faculty before they get more job security is to document a pattern of turnover, which hopefully can be used as evidence in the grievance process.

In Daniel B. Davis' book, *Contingent Academic Labor: Evaluating Conditions to Improve Student Outcomes*, some of the issues I have discussed in this chapter are addressed through the development of a "Contingent Labor Conditions Scorecard" (100). The main categories in the scorecard that Davis uses for assessment of labor practices are:

1. Material equity: Pay parity, job security, and benefits
2. Professional equity: Professional opportunity and professional identity
3. Social equity: inclusiveness of gender and race

In looking at the first category of material equity, the UC-AFT contract represents a middle ground between TT positions and fully at-will contingent ones. While NTT faculty jobs in the UC system do offer some level of security, they are not as secure as tenured positions. Additionally, even though the UC system does not provide pay parity between NTT faculty and tenured professors, within the national contingent ranks, the pay offered by the UC system is at the higher end. However, UC system NTT positions only provide full benefits and a pension for faculty working at least half-time, which means there are many part-time workers who are not included.

When it comes to the second category of professional equity, although contingent faculty members in the UC system can apply for professional development funding, the support they receive is not as generous as it is for their tenured colleagues. In short, these positions offer a middle ground between pure contingency and tenure. For people with a more radical vision, the in-between status of these contingent positions may seem unappealing and merely a way of compromising with the system; however, I believe that more equitable working conditions can be fought for if partial victories are achieved first. Contingent faculty and their allies can then build on these successes to increase collective power. In the next chapter, I discuss some of the methods individuals and groups can use to fight for better working conditions for all NTT faculty.

Chapter 3. Organizing for Change

This chapter outlines different ways that contingent faculty have organized to make their workplaces more democratic and just. The goal here is to examine actual practices and how they have come into being, such as those described by Ashley Dawson in relation to the City University of New York in her article "Another University is Possible," and to offer a guide to collective organizing in both unionized and non-unionized settings. I begin with a discussion of the basic aspects of organizing, and then I move on to specific examples of NTT faculty members working together to improve their working conditions. It is important to stress that my main audience in this chapter is contingent faculty members and organizers who are dedicated to improving the employment situation of teachers who are not eligible for tenure.

The first key to building a more democratic workplace is to fight against the notion that only certain faculty can perform specific functions. To break away from this class and caste system, precarious faculty should start with the principle that their employment status should not determine their role in shared governance. Even when an institution does discriminate against faculty based on whether they are eligible for tenure or not, contingent faculty should believe that they have the right to participate as equal members of a shared community (Dawson 99). At times, this attitude requires demanding equal voting power through an appeal to democratic principles. In other words, just as we argue "no taxation without representation," we should also argue "no work without shared governance." Of course, this may be an impossible ideal, but it can function to change the mindset of workers who are used to being controlled and managed in an authoritarian manner.

It is important to remember that one reason why contingent faculty often have little say over their working conditions is that tenured professors are afraid of giving the NTT faculty power (Kezar et al., "Challenging Stereotypes" 130). From this perspective, the people in power are on the defensive, and this means that they are vulnerable to the collective force of the disempowered. For instance, when part-time teachers are told that they cannot attend faculty meetings, they can demand inclusion, and if they are rejected, they can consider just showing up and presenting a collective front. Of course, the fear is that they will lose their jobs for acting in such a "disrespectful" way, but contingent faculty need to realize that the department is dependent on their labor, and if people stick together, it is highly unlikely that they will all be let go. When people occupy a space as an act of resistance, they show that they belong there and that they are not willing to be ignored (Jansen 40). My experience is that each time workers engage in a collective action like this, they gain a stronger sense of their power, which makes them fight for more justice and fairer treatment, much as described in Jason A. Ostrander et al.'s "Collective Power to Create Political Change." Sometimes all it takes is a group of faculty writing a letter together; the key is that people see that they have power and that they can work with others to organize their power in a collective manner.

In terms of higher education, contingent faculty members need to influence how people are hired, how they are assessed, how budgets are spent, how classes are distributed, and how decisions are made in general. The NTT faculty can demand to be on all committees and to have full voting rights, and, as Keith Hoeller suggests in "The Future of the Contingent Faculty Movement," they should also fight to have their work compensated on an equal basis. If a certain institutional rule prohibits their full participation, they can fight to change it, and they should shame professors and administrators for not living up to their own liberal standards of justice. In other words, they need to fight for the democratization of their workplace, and this requires seeing their institution as a place organized around democratic principles, even when, as Karl E. Klare points out, it is not (68–69). I have found that shaming tactics usually do not work well when negotiating contracts, but they can be effective when dealing with people who are trying to manage the reputations of their institutions or their own careers.

Some professors and administrators may argue that NTT faculty members do not have the time or expertise to participate in shared governance, but the response of the contingent faculty should be to demand the time and training to be able to participate as full citizens of their academic community. What I am stressing here is that contingent workers have to first change their mindset before they can change their workplaces since they need to see themselves as worthy of full democratic participation. Even if their department or college is far from being democratic, it is important to demand democracy whenever possible.

● The Power of Not Working

My experience in bargaining with university officials over the terms and conditions of contingent academic work shows that the main thing administrators want is to maintain the status quo and keep everything running as smoothly as possible. The reason, then, why strikes and other forms of work stoppages can be so effective is because they disrupt the smooth functioning of the administrative machine as they open a space for people to think about doing things differently (Godard 169n14). Even if one is in a state that does not allow collective bargaining agreements or strikes, there is no way to stop workers from meeting together and engaging in a wide range of collective activities. The first step is that employees have to see themselves as worthy of power, and then they have to find ways of working with others to gain more control over their working lives.

It is often important to seek out allies in order to enhance a group's power, and for contingent faculty, this often means finding non-contingent faculty who will support the cause of precarious academic workers because "tenured faculty do still wield considerable power on many of our campuses" (Betensky). While this process of gaining allies can be frustrating and disappointing at times, it is important to get liberal and progressive faculty to see how their ideals should be applied to their own workplaces. I have found that potential allies are often simply ignorant of what is going on in their own departments, or they have blindly bought into a system of prejudice. In fact, by getting the TT faculty to see the devaluation of contingent faculty as a form of discrimination, they may be more likely to join a group or sign a petition. As many organizers know, it often starts with one small act, which then can lead to other more ambitious actions (Alinsky).

It is also vital to see how a group or union needs to form a coalition with other groups that may appear at first to have little common cause (Eaton 408). For instance, in the UC-AFT union's push to have a tax on the wealthy to support higher education in California, the union worked with immigrant groups, groups fighting for prison reform, and people focused on LGBTQ rights. All of these different collective organizations had a desire to protect public institutions, and they realized that their power was enhanced when they worked with other groups, even when those groups had a different central focus. Coalitions are most effective when they realize that they can gain influence and leverage by working on issues that are adjacent to their own (Dyke 226). In this structure, when janitors come out to support contingent teachers, the janitors know that when they need support, the teachers will be there for them (Carter et al.).

The problem with many coalitions is that the different groups are sometimes unable to give up their focus on their own main issues in order to help out another group, and this often leads to infighting and a lack of unity (Kelly 721). What the coalition needs to concentrate on is building long-term collective power so the victory of one member group can lead to the enhanced future power of the other related groups (Levkoe 176). In the case of contingent faculty, this process of coalition building at times has been hindered by a narrow focus on specific, immediate problems, which blocks access to a more long-term, strategic approach.

Contingent faculty are also hard to organize because many simply have little time since they are working multiple jobs and have other important commitments (Levkoe 178). To overcome this issue, it is important to discover what people are willing to do—even if what they can do appears to be minimal. This process requires people actually talking to other people, and this can be hard to do if contingent faculty do not have offices or time to meet. However, meeting in person is necessary for building solidarity, and so if nothing else, organizers should seek out teachers in their classrooms to see if they are willing to talk. This strategy is what Gladys McKenzie and Kris Rondeau used at the University of Minnesota when organizing workers there (Oppenheim 51–52).

● The Organizing Conversation

The first conversation with someone who is not involved in the collective movement to increase workplace democracy and improve working conditions usually centers on simply letting the new person say what they do not like about their current job. Once this person feels they have been listened to without judgment, the next stage is to simply ask if they would be willing to meet again or go to a meeting. The important thing is not to begin with telling them what they need to do and asking them to engage in an activity they may find risky or burdensome; instead, the organizer has to slowly build the relationship based on mutual understanding and respect (Yates).

After a contingent faculty member shows a willingness to take the first step and attend a meeting, it is vital to give that person something to do so that their connection to the organization will be sustained. A key focus of all meetings should be the building of a sense of community by helping faculty see that their issues are recognized and shared by other people. It is also important to point to examples of success in overcoming problems in order to give people hope that change is possible. What organizers should avoid is turning a meeting into a session of mere complaining; problems should be recognized, but they also should be tied to possible solutions (Bronfenbrenner at al.).

Much of what I have been discussing revolves around a change in perspective, and this is more about psychology than pure politics. Employees have to believe that their work is important and that they are stronger as a collective than as individuals. They also have to feel that they are being heard and that their issues matter to other people. My experience is that it is important to focus on these basic elements of organizing because most academic workers do not have much knowledge about building collective democratic organizations (Markowitz n.p.). In fact, one problem with many unions is that they tend to be undemocratic and top-down because most of the workers do not have the time or the resources to be involved in a very active way. However, if we want our workplaces to be more democratic, we have to model democracy in our own collective organizations (Turner and Hurd 9).

Making a collective group democratic does not mean that there is no leadership or structure; rather, there has to be a constant effort to get everyone involved in every activity so that people do not feel alienated. Many academic organizations suffer because only a few people do most of the work, while the vast majority of members cede power to people with the loudest voices or the most experience. At all times, the goal should be to model an effective form of democracy that will make people feel their voices matter (Johnston). It is also important to guard against activist fatigue, which occurs when all of the work falls on just a few of the members.

Since contingent faculty are often rightfully afraid of losing their jobs, it is important to stress the protections gained through being part of a collective. This can be achieved by constantly referring to the power of the group and the importance of its labor. People have to believe that the other members of the group will have their backs in tough times, and they have to move from a sense of being vulnerable to a sense of being powerful. Of course, this will not always work, and some people may lose their jobs when they engage in collective action, but the group needs to defend these displaced workers through a constant signaling of solidarity, which can be enhanced through the development of a strike fund.

● Bargaining Versus Organizing

One big issue I have seen in my own union experience is that people do not understand that organizing and bargaining are often two different things with distinct processes and priorities. Organizers try to build solidarity among a group, and this often requires an "us vs. them" mentality, which is because the people in the group need to have a defined grievance and a defined enemy (Melucci). This binary logic helps to solidify the group around a set of demands that are made to the people with power, but since this method of organizing requires a focus on emotion and antagonism, it can subvert the ultimate goal of working with the other side to achieve a fair and reasonable outcome. From this perspective, bargaining requires a more rational and less antagonistic approach because one has to negotiate with the group that was previously represented as the enemy, a practice illustrated by Harry C. Katz et al. (587–88). If in organizing one seeks to shame the other side, in bargaining, one has to see those on the other side as equals working for a common good.

This conflict between organizing and bargaining occurs in all groups, not just unions (Doellgast and Benassi). Whenever a collective seeks to have a wrong addressed, it needs to first rally around a grievance in order to gain power to negotiate as a unified front. However, even if the group with the demands thinks the other side is the cause of its problems, it is usually ineffective to try to come to an agreement with a group for which the aggrieved group does not have respect or trust. Therefore, a transition has to be made between organizing and bargaining in order to build that respect and trust, and this switch mirrors the difference Amy Gutmann and Dennis Thompson describe between campaigning and governing (xiii-xv). While recent strikes by K-12 teachers in Chicago and Los Angeles have shown that organizing and negotiating can be combined in an effective manner, it still important to see how these two aspects of collective organizing can move in opposite directions.

If we look at the history of minority-based social movements, we see that often they first rally around a shared trauma and identity, but their ultimate goal is to be included into a system of equal justice (Zinn). Once again, there is a conflict between the means and the ends since the way a group gains solidarity is by focusing on their particularity, yet what it aims to achieve is based on universality (Butler et al.). In other words, paradoxically, a group that sees itself as different has to demand to be treated the same as others. As we shall see in the next chapter, one of the biggest stumbling blocks for gaining more respect and better treatment for contingent faculty is the way they are often represented by the people who want to help them.

● Alternative Models of Organizing for Collective Power

While it is evident that the most effective way to improve the working conditions of contingent faculty is through unionization, it is vital to look at alternative modes of organizing since many faculty work in states that do not sanction collective bargaining (Kezar et al., *Gig Academy* 121). We can gain a sense of some of the ways precarious faculty have sought to improve their jobs on a collective basis both with and without union support by examining examples from the edited collection *Contingency, Exploitation, and Solidarity: Labor and Action in English Composition*; all the examples in the following subsections come from this book. For instance, in the chapter "Silent Subversion, Quiet Competence, and Patient Persistence," we see how a few NTT faculty members began a process of gaining a course release by first meeting with their chair as a group (Lind and Mullin 14). In other words, they did not use a formal organization to push for a desired change; instead, they simply met together with someone who had a certain amount of authority in their workplace.

These contingent faculty members decided to write a formal proposal, which they later presented to the chair (Lind and Mullin 17). This very process of collectively producing a document can be seen as a part of organizing for more democratic power since it required individual teachers to enter into a collaborative process directed towards a group concern. As is common of a bottom-up effort, they were not guided by an external organization or any formal structure; rather, they worked together to take matters into their own hands by crafting a collective demand (Macy and Flache). The chair suggested ways that they could improve their document (Lind and Mullin 18), and here we see the power of people self-organizing and creating a productive relationship with someone who held the power to effectuate change. Although these actions may seem small and insignificant, each collective effort has the possibility of producing a sense of group agency, which fights against a sense of isolation and despair.

The next stage in this process involved creating a committee to oversee the process of distributing class releases to the NTT faculty, and this group included "the department chair, the associate chair, the director of the writing program, and one NTT" faculty member (Lind and Mullin 18). In creating a committee with the inclusion of a contingent faculty person, we see the importance of using academic structures to enhance the power and recognition of precarious teachers. While some people see committee work as dreaded service, this type of activity can represent a key way of augmenting the power and status of contingent faculty (Kezar and Lester). In fact, every time a structure is produced that pushes tenured and NTT faculty to work together on a common goal, the possibility for improving the working conditions of contingent faculty increases (Rhoades, "Creative Leveraging"). This does not mean that the process will always be successful, but the more people work together, the less likely the dominating group will be able to treat the subordinate group with indifference or ignorance.

O Creating an Advocacy Group

Another way that contingent faculty can organize to improve their working conditions without the aid of a union is through the formation of an advocacy group
(Jolley et al.). In their chapter, "Despair Is Not an Option," Anna K. Nardo and Barbara Heifferon describe how, after their local union at Louisiana State University
separated itself from the national union, some of the faculty decided to form an
independent organization that focused on going to monthly board of supervisor
meetings in order to present their issues during the public comment part of the
sessions; since they knew that the press would be covering these events, they felt
they had a good chance to expose their grievances to the general public (38). In
fact, once the chancellor responded to some of the comments by calling for a salary increase for all faculty, the people involved in the group were able to use their
victory to call for more secure positions for contingent faculty (39).

This example demonstrates that when faculty members work together to
make a grievance public, they can sometimes put enough pressure on their
administration to extract concessions. We learn from the title of their chapter
that despair is not the solution but that people must organize and agitate for
better working conditions. It is also vital to stress that when an advocacy group
is formed, it is hard to predict how successful it will be or what will happen in the
future, yet the mere act of creating a collective organization can help to transform the psychology of the people who feel oppressed by the system (Whittier).
By creating a new community with a set purpose and strategy, people are motivated to move from a position of helpless victimization to one of empowered
involvement. As Nardo and Heifferon note about the situation on their campus,
"Respect and advocacy have helped restore morale, returned stability to the core
writing faculty, and made substantial progress toward concrete improvements
in employment conditions" (39). While these advocates did not get everything
they wanted, they were able to improve both their working conditions and their
state of mind, which should not be discounted.

O Working Inside and Outside of the Union

In their chapter, "An Apologia and a Way Forward: In Defense of the Lecturer
Line in Writing Programs," Mark McBeth and Tim McCormack illustrate how
local advocacy can take advantage of a union contract by fighting for specific
solutions to particular programmatic needs. They describe how, by enlisting the
help of a new writing program administrator, contingent faculty members at
John Jay College were able to transform many part-time positions into full-time,
non-tenure track jobs (54). Part of the way that they advocated for this transformation was through organizing around new curricular changes that were being
demanded by the English department leadership (43). Since they knew that they
would not be able to change how their courses were taught without a more stable faculty who had the time and support to learn the new curriculum, they

were able to successfully ask the administration for several full-time, non-tenure track lines, which were defined by the following requirements:

- Lecturers hold full-time positions within the English department, with the potential of a Certificate of Continued Employment [hereafter, CCE] in their fifth year, as provided by the union contract;
- Lecturers earn one course of reassigned time in their first year to take a teaching practicum seminar;
- Lecturers have a constructive and progressive agenda of service to the writing program, the department, and the college;
- Lecturers will go through faculty review and promotion processes of annual review by the chair and submission of a Form C; however, these evaluations will focus only on teaching and service;
- Lecturers are assessed by the P&B committee based on their teaching observations, their student evaluations, their pedagogical and curricular contributions, and their service to the writing program, department, or college;
- Lecturers are eligible for promotional steps to associate and full lecturer … ;
- Lecturers may apply for sabbaticals after attaining the CCE and 6 years of full-time service;
- Lecturers have departmental voting rights, office space, and travel funds in the same way that tenure-track faculty do;
- Lecturers are eligible for the same reassigned time as tenure-track faculty, based on service contributions to the writing program, the department, or the college;
- Lecturers can apply for fellowships, grants, and other non-teaching opportunities and have access to reassigned time for college or departmental service in the same manner as full-time faculty (49; square brackets in the original).

These position are very similar to the ones in the UC system that I described in the previous chapter; however, one of the interesting additions is the requirement that contingent faculty members earn reassigned time in the first year to take a teaching practicum. Because the new curriculum would require faculty to be trained to teach in a specific way, the program was able to argue for improved working conditions in the form of compensatory time for professional development. It is interesting to note that the authors discuss that some of the faculty members were against these positions because, similar to the stance of the American Association of University Professors, they wanted to protect tenure and thought that the creation of full-time, non-tenure track faculty would only serve to create a new class of exploited workers (45–47). However, McBeth and McCormack argue that when these positions are constructed with care, they can offer an effective middle-ground between tenure and total contingency:

By listing specific work criteria and explicit benefits, we defined the positions as equal to tenure-track positions; lecturers would have additional teaching and service contributions in place of the scholarship and publishing responsibilities of TT faculty. By outlining lecturers' equal access to the benefits and opportunities of full-time faculty, we also circumvented concerns of our tenure-track colleagues who worried about a two-caste full-time professoriate. (49)

The fact of the matter is that this type of position is growing, so it is essential to make sure that these contingent positions are structured in a more fair and equitable manner (Drake et al.). This example also focuses attention on the need to make sure that the hiring processes for FTNTT faculty positions approximate the rigorous requirements for TT hires (Kezar, "Needed Policies" 4). McBeth and McCormack address how they handled this:

To further allay the perception that there is a two-tier faculty, and as a means to insure a competitive hiring process, we asked applicants to meet rigorous candidacy requirements equal to our tenure-track hires. Each applicant submitted a philosophy of teaching, a course syllabus they had taught, and a prospective course they could teach, as well as examples of their teaching practice. All candidates completed a qualifying interview, and a full-day campus visit. (50)

One of the best ways to assure that contingent positions will be treated with respect and dignity is to make sure that the hiring process is seen by the tenured faculty as being as demanding as TT searches.

McBeth and McCormack make the important argument that FTNTT positions often a middle ground that undermines the institutional binary pitting the tenured faculty against adjuncts and note that

we see the mistake of manufacturing a binary labor division between fully-employed, happy tenure-track faculty and underemployed, unhappy, part-time faculty. At John Jay College, if we had retained this either-or vision, we would not have gained the qualified writing program faculty that we can boast today, and those faculty would have remained on the low-status spinning wheel of "adjunctland." (53)

The type of advocacy promoted by these faculty members revolves around a pragmatic vision that eschews binary thinking or the hope for a complete revolution; instead, they illustrate that positive social change often involves finding ways to work within the system and transforming the system from the inside (Henig and Stone).

O Is This a Workable Compromise?

As mentioned above, the number of FTNTT positions are increasing faster than TT positions in many fields. In fact, in their chapter, "Real Faculty But Not: The

Full-Time, Non-Tenure-Track Position as Contingent Labor," Richard Colby and Rebekah Shultz Colby discuss how this transformation is reshaping higher education. They note a 2008 MLA report showing "that while tenure-track faculty employment . . . increased 5 percent between 1995 and 2005, FTNTT positions [showed] a 40 percent increase and adjunct faculty a 38 percent increase during that same time" (58). They also note the American Association of University Professors reports this trend "is also true across departments" (58). Therefore, due to the tremendous increase in these contingent positions, it is essential for faculty to figure out how to make them as fair and equitable as possible.

As Colby and Colby insist, one way to enhance these jobs is to make sure that contingent faculty members are able to participate in the same range of activities as tenured faculty. In looking at their home institution of the University of Denver and others, they highlight that "many FTNTT positions provide faculty opportunities to sit on faculty senates, participate in advising students, direct programs, or share in the governance of the writing programs to which they belong, and, most importantly, to provide comparable if not better instruction to students than TT faculty" (59). The main point here is that instead of fearing the loss of tenure, a better strategy might be to see how we can make full-time, non-tenure track positions even more effective and just than TT ones (Levin and Shaker).

The University of Denver model seeks to enhance these FTNTT contingent faculty positions by providing a quarter off each year for "programmatic research, writing center work, or [teaching] a first-year seminar based on a research interest" and by providing "$1,000 a year for conference expenses" and "$500 each year for professional development" (60). Since this department is largely self-governed, the FTNTT faculty have a central role in developing curriculum, but the director still retains a great deal of power (60). Colby and Colby affirm that while these positions are not perfect, they represent a dramatic improvement over the past:

> For those who have worked as adjuncts, the FTNTT position can offer security of employment, benefits, a living wage, and time to develop professionally and pedagogically. Furthermore, as an academic couple with newly minted Ph.D.s, we counted ourselves lucky to have found positions where one or both of us did not have to commute for hours to work as adjuncts at multiple institutions. (61)

One lesson to be drawn from this example is that we should not let the perfect be the enemy of the good as we work to steadily improve the working conditions of NTT faculty. By using a pragmatic approach, these contingent workers were able to work with their director to create positive social change as they focused on professional development and democratic participation in workplace decisions. However, it is important to point out that these FTNTT faculty were in part dependent on the good will of a tenured administrator who was sympathetic to their cause and acted as a buffer between the faculty and the higher administration. Therefore, another lesson to draw from this example is that it is often necessary to work with tenured faculty and administrators who are willing to improve the status and support for contingent faculty. Therefore, instead of simply demonizing tenured professors and administrators, it is often essential to form alliances and work together in the formation of collective agency.

○ Converting Contingency

A possible alternative to simply working within the system and trying to use collective organizing to improve the status and working conditions of contingent faculty is to create a path for NTT faculty to convert to TT positions; some argue that conversion is the best possible option (Besosa et al. 90). This process is documented by Lalicker and Lynch-Biniek in their chapter "Contingency, Solidarity, and Community Building: Principles for Converting Contingent to Tenure Track." Drawing from their experience working in the Pennsylvania State System of Higher Education (PASSHE), where they are represented by the Association of Pennsylvania State College and University Faculty (APSCUF) union, these authors outline a system where each department develops a procedure to convert temporary positions to the tenure track (91).

Lalicker and Lynch-Biniek offer several key principles for making these conversions possible and effective as they show how a system-wide contract provision can result in very different outcomes according to the local community and departmental culture. The first principle they present is the need to hire faculty with real expertise in their discipline, explaining that since the conversion to a TT position will require the assessment of disciplinary knowledge, it is essential to hire contingent faculty who will have a good chance at passing a tenure review (93). Moreover, another principle they suggest is that the hiring process should mirror as much as possible the process that is used to search for and hire TT faculty (95). In other words, if you want to give contingent faculty the best chance at attaining tenure, you have to plan ahead at the start and make sure that the people you hire will have the credentials and the expertise that will help them pass a rigorous tenure review process. One benefit of this system is that it encourages departments to stop relying on last-minute hires of under-qualified people (95).

Furthermore, another principle suggested by Lalicker and Lynch-Biniek is to make sure that contingent faculty will have their past years of service counted towards their tenure clock (96). Similarly it is necessary to provide FTNTT faculty with opportunities for professional development and committee work (96). In order to give contingent faculty the best chance at being converted, Lalicker and Lynch-Biniek explain it is important to "maximize contingent faculty access to the complete collegial life of the department: meetings, policy discussions, social events, scholarly discussions, committee service and funding for professional development" (96). In other words, all contingent faculty should be treated as equals, and they should be given the same opportunity to involve themselves in all collegial activities.

Not only should opportunities for involvement exist, but, according to another principle advanced by Lalicker and Lynch-Biniek, assessment of FTNTT and TT faculty members alike should be based on teaching, research, and service (97). The great potential of this system is that even if a particular faculty member does not gain conversion, each contingent worker is treated in a more equitable way. We also see here the power of breaking down the strict binary between tenure-track and non-tenure track faculty. If all faculty are required to do instruction, service, and research, then it is hard to maintain a strict hierarchy and system of oppression (Mbuva 94).

One way of breaking down hierarchies and combining organizing with service is through the process of mentoring new faculty. By assigning tenured faculty members to work with contingent faculty, both people are pushed to learn from each other and develop expertise together. As Lalicker and Lynch-Biniek argue in yet another principle, mentorship is a vital way to build a collegial community, which can lead to a more just and equitable workplace (99).

O Faculty Bill of Rights

For faculty who do not have a union or who have a union that does not fight for the protections of contingent faculty, one possible path to improved working conditions through collective action is the formation of an academic bill of rights, which can be voted on by the faculty senate. As we see in Rolf Norgaard's "The Uncertain Future of Past Success: Memory, Narrative, and the Dynamics of Institutional Change," faculty at the University of Colorado-Boulder in 1993 used the shared governance system to pass a document called the "Instructors' Bill of Rights," which included the following stipulations:

- Lecturers working for three years at 50 percent appointments or greater should be appointed as full-time instructors.
- Instructors should have multi-year, presumptively renewable appointments, ranging from two to four years, with three years being the default term.
- The typical workload for instructors was defined as three courses per semester (3/3 for the academic year), with a merit evaluation ratio of 75 percent teaching and 25 percent service. (Tenure-stream faculty generally teach a 2/2 load, with merit evaluations of 40 percent research, 40 percent teaching, and 20 percent service.)
- The floor for starting salaries for full-time instructors was set, at the time, at $30K (instructors are merit-pool eligible).
- After seven years in rank, instructors would be eligible for promotion to senior instructor.
- Senior instructors are eligible for a semester of reduced teaching load after every seven years of full-time teaching for purposes of pedagogical and curricular research. (135)

This system was designed to create a clear career path for contingent faculty while recognizing the different employment situation of TT and NTT faculty.

It also aimed to set minimums for salaries and establish a merit review process.

Interestingly, as Norgaard explains, Colorado is a right-to-work state, so the agreement with the university covering these positions is not protected by a union, and there is spotty adherence to the agreement's provisions (136). Although it is clear that this lack of the enforcement coming from a collective bargaining agreement makes this arrangement more vulnerable, it does allow us to think about how to organize in states where union protections are not possible. Instead of simply positing, as Thomas Auxter does, that unionization is the only real way to organize, we have to take a pragmatic approach and develop multiple modes of collective organizing to improve the working conditions of contingent faculty.

Norgaard argues that since the FTNTT positions at the University of Colorado-Boulder did not require or reward research, professional development had to be tied to different forms of service:

> Were it not for instructor service, residential academic programs in the residence halls and service-learning initiatives would not have been possible. Indeed, given that instructor appointments did not require (nor did they explicitly reward) research, service became the contractual space that permitted professional development, conference presentations, grant writing, and publishing. Thanks to this service component, instructors gained influence with administrators and began playing an active role in campus-wide faculty governance. (136)

Like the University of California's system contract for lecturers, the University of Colorado-Boulder structure uses the category of service to help expand beyond teaching the expectations of NTT faculty, and this expansion allows for more involvement in shared governance and a host of other activities.

One of Norgaard's key points is that since the "Instructors' Bill of Rights" was not binding, it was up to the faculty to constantly remind administrators of its existence (137). Therefore, he argues that part of organizing is making sure that the "institutional memory" is kept alive, and this process often entails contingent faculty involving themselves in departmental and university-wide governance (137). One lesson here is that the work of organizing never ends, so it is essential to develop a sustainable collective organization. Ideally, this organization would be a union with collective bargaining rights, but in our current political system, sometimes it is necessary to settle for a more tenuous form of collective power.

O Writing to Right a Wrong

As we have seen throughout this chapter, organizing can occur in many different forms, so we should be open to a flexible model of collective action. For example, in their chapter, "Non-Tenure Track Activism: Genre Appropriation in Program Reporting," Chris Blankenship and Justin M. Jory describe how a group of NTT faculty at the University of Colorado at Colorado Springs worked together to produce a report that countered an official report made for a seven-year external program review (152). This group collaboratively created an alternative description of the needs and working conditions of these precarious laborers, and then they presented their own document to the external reviewers, and they made sure that each NTT faculty member would talk to the reviewers about particular areas of concern (157). Here we see one of the ways outlined by Nhung Pham and Valerie Osland Paton that an informal group can insert themselves into a formal process in order to make sure their issues are confronted.

As described by Blankenship and Jory, the report written by the NTT faculty led to a series of meetings between TT and NTT faculty, meetings that were made less contentious through the use of Robert's Rules of Order[6] and the presence of the dean (158). This process eventually resulted in the contingent faculty gaining governance rights in their department for the first time (159). While this inclusion of NTT faculty produced much conflict and resistance (160–63), we should expect nothing less from a process calling for a more equal distribution of resources and power. Sometimes the very resistances that seem to block progress help to build a sense of solidarity amongst the workers trying to improve their working conditions. Moreover, as the situation described by Blankenship and Jory reveals, it is often necessary to play both an inside and outside game in the sense that one has to use internal processes, such as writing and submitting a report, while one agitates from an external position (Jarzabkowski and Fenton).

● The Future of Empowering Contingent Faculty

One of my aims of this chapter has been to explore the many different ways contingent faculty can work together to improve their working conditions, much as Joe Berry does in *Reclaiming the Ivory Tower: Organizing Adjuncts to Change Higher Education*. As we have seen, when it comes to organizing, there is no one-size-fits-all solution that works in every situation. However, what should be clear is that when NTT faculty work together to improve their plight, they can create a more democratic and just workplace. Yet, as we shall see in the next two chapters, some of the major resistances to this movement for positive social change comes from the very people who want to help improve the situation.

---

6. For details about Robert's Rules of Order, see *Robert's Rules of Order Revised for Deliberative Assemblies* by Henry Martyn Robert.

Chapter 4. Countering Prejudices

In his book *The Adjunct Underclass*, Herb Childress reiterates many of the common perceptions about how contingent faculty are treated today:

> There are innumerable terms in use for the vast army of temp labor within higher ed–adjunct faculty, part-time lecturer, visiting scholar, postdoctoral fellow, professor of the practice, artist in residence. They all mask the unified underlying condition: working course-by-course or year-by-year, with no guarantee of permanence, often for embarrassingly small stipends, and often for no benefits. The polite language makes the facts harder to see, so let's state it simply: College teaching has become primarily a pickup job, like driving for Uber or running chores for TaskRabbit. (5)

Although I believe it would be wrong to deny that many–if not most–precarious faculty are faced with the conditions Childress describes, it is counterproductive to overgeneralize and thereby exclude contingent faculty who have very different working conditions. Not only does Childress' representation serve to reiterate destructive stereotypes, but by denying the existence of more progressive alternatives, it may undermine the desire of people to fight for better working conditions, as Kezar and her colleagues describe can happen in "Challenging Stereotypes That Interfere with Effective Governance."

As I have shown in my descriptions of the working conditions for contingent academic labor in the UC system and other institutions, not every contingent faculty member is hired on a short-term basis, and many do have access to benefits and professional development funding. Therefore, by ignoring some of the better working conditions for contingent faculty, Childress' portrayal may rob adjunct faculty of any hope that things can improve, and it also may send the message to administrators and tenured faculty, many of whom mistakenly believe that higher education is a meritocracy (Schwartz 506), that this category of workers should only be treated in a negative way. In fact, on numerous occasions, I have had to tell professors and administrators that the contingent faculty members they work with don't just teach and that they are not all hired on a course-by-course basis. Even in departments that are staffed by mostly NTT lecturers, some professors deny the situation and only see contingent faculty through the same overgeneralizations that Childress reiterates.

It is important to stress that we need to recognize the bad treatment of precarious academic labor that Childress presents, but we should not be blinded by overgeneralizations that reinforce stereotypes and prejudices and that can serve to naturalize contingent social constructions. In other words, people should know that things can be different. For instance, the following statement from Childress does not allow for a recognition of the diversity of working conditions for contingent faculty: "Academia essentially lays off all of its contingent employees at the end of each contract" (13). Once again, it is true that many precarious faculty are hired only on a short-term basis, but this is the worst practice that is countered by many other contractual arrangements and institutional policies and practices (Maxey and Kezar).[7]

As I have documented in my depiction of the UC system and other institutions, contingent faculty can earn continuing appointments with no end date, and in situations like this, they can be hired for at least one year at a time during their probationary period. There is thus a middle ground between tenured faculty and the type of faculty that Childress describes, yet he never addresses this alternative. Instead, he insists,

> There is a second order of the faculty class, though . . . : the non-tenure-track or NTT faculty. They differ from the TT in several ways. There is no expectation of permanence; indeed, the expectation is for impermanence, for contracts lasting from one course in one semester to a few years at most. NTT faculty do not set curricula, and may not even set the syllabus for their own courses, instead delivering a standard package designed by others. They are not supported to teach and do research, but instead do one or the other exclusively. They typically get little or no professional development, nor are they supported for conference travel, professional memberships, or publication expenses. (20)

I know for a fact that thousands of contingent faculty inside and outside of the UC system have working conditions that counter every aspect of Childress' description; for example, I have helped other unions write contracts that give contingent faculty continuing appointments, professional development funding, and academic freedom rights (Rhoades and Maitland). Unfortunately, it is very difficult to find reliable data on how many faculty work under particular conditions, and although admirable work has been done on trying to document this information, one really has to look at the facts on the ground to see what is really happening.[8] I hope this book contributes to this process by giving detailed descriptions of actual practices. If we do not do this work, people will be left thinking that contingent faculty members only teach courses designed by others.

I fear that by focusing on the worst situations, activists such as Childress participate in a form of victim identity that limits the hope for progressive social change (Cole 7). For instance, in the following passage, Childress disregards the important contributions to academic research and service that many contingent faculty make on a daily basis and instead portrays contingent faculty as victims:

---

7. A long list of books and articles document the exploitative treatment of precarious academic labor. Some of the most important works are Nelson; Ross; Giroux; Bousquet, *How the University*; Donoghue; Lee and Kahn; and Slaughter and Rhoades.

8. For research on the diverse working conditions of contingent faculty, see Spaniel and Scott; Donhardt and Layden; and Boldt.

"What they can't provide is a substantial contribution to the larger academic discourse within which they were trained. NTTs are content providers accomplishing a constrained task" (21). However, unlike Childress, who sees things in an extreme black-and-white way, we have to look at the complexity and diversity of actual working conditions. It has been my experience that administrators often use the argument that contingent faculty only teach to justify paying them less and excluding them from other benefits and responsibilities. For example, I have had to correct many institutional documents in the UC system that wrongly claim NTT lecturers are assessed only for their teaching. The truth is that lecturers often are evaluated also for their service and professional development. My fear is that one reason why university officials are able to ignore what is happening in their own institutions is that they rely on the type of stereotypes that Childress and others continue to circulate.

At one point in his book, Childress does appear to present a more complex and nuanced representation of NTT faculty:

> Nationwide, data collected by the *Chronicle of Higher Education* shows more than half of the full-timers are themselves impermanent, hired for limited terms with no expectation of renewal, not welcomed into the larger conversations of institutional mission. The American Association of University Professors shows a different proportion, with about a third of full-timers being NTT. Either way, colleges have a large block of faculty who live in a middle ground of contingency, a community claimed as members when the institution wants to look good to accreditors and renounced when it comes time to grant them the privileges of TT life. (23)

On the one hand, Childress does acknowledge the fact that not all precarious faculty are part-time, but on the other hand, he quickly dismisses the value of these positions. As seen in the following passage, his rejection of the importance of FTNTT positions is due to his over-generalized and stereotypical way of seeing these jobs:

> Although the full-time NTT have little say in the design of courses or the larger curricula within which they fit, they are often given some administrative work to do (in exchange for a twelve-month contract, meaning that their summers are no longer available for the research and writing they might otherwise have taken up as part of their career development). (26)

This claim that contingent faculty have little say in the development of their courses is countered by the fact that many NTT faculty inside and outside of the UC system develop their own courses (Elman; Thompson, "Contingent Faculty"; and Ehrenberg 195). To deny this fact is to dismiss and belittle the labor of thousands of faculty members.

My point here is not to single out Childress for his stereotypical representation of contingent faculty; rather, I view his work as indicative of a very common way of seeing NTT faculty in a very limited and negative manner. Of course, his intention is to reveal the bad treatment of these teachers in order to help them make a claim for better working conditions, but by ignoring the reality of the diversity and complexity of these positions, he cannot help but reinforce the worst negative depictions of these positions. For instance, in the following passage, he repeats some of the most destructive views regarding undergraduate teaching, and as we shall see, it is often hard to determine if he is stating what he thinks other people think or if he actually has internalized these negative views:

> Writing instruction is highly reliant on contingent faculty, as are lower-division math courses, science-for-nonmajors "breadth courses," and introductory social science and humanities courses. These are the courses that are treated as commodities, one product being the same as any other, produced and consumed in every landscape, teachable by faculty with less specialization and expertise. The departments often disparagingly refer to them as "service courses"–courses that fulfill larger institutional needs rather than being explicitly for students within their majors, and which thus don't deserve precious departmental resources. (78)

Although it is true that some faculty and administrators do consider required undergraduate courses to be less valuable, many other people see them as essential.[9] However, by only representing the most negative view, Childress simply re-circulates a destructive stereotype and prejudice.

A major reason for Childress' unintentional destructive discourse is that, like so many others, he uses hyperbolic language and has a tendency to overgeneralize and represent issues in a stark black-and-white manner. We see this unnuanced stance in the next passage, in which he continues to represent the situation of contingent faculty in the most negative and extreme ways as he discusses diversity, equity, and inclusion initiatives in higher education:

> These initiatives of contemporary higher ed work both for and against students, because it's almost certain that the enormous contingent faculty won't be welcome to participate in any of them. Adjuncts won't be invited to the professional development workshops about community-engaged learning, won't be invited to include their students as research partners in their (unfunded and often nonexistent) scholarly endeavors. They won't be paid to attend safe-space training for LGBTQ+ support, or to attend workshops about support for autistic students. They won't even know the array of resources available to students on their campuses. (95–96)

---

9. I explore these perceptions of undergraduate education in Samuels, *The Politics of Writing Studies.*

What Childress does not acknowledge is, as in the case of the UC system, some institutions do fund NTT faculty for professional development and institutional service (Kezar and Lester). Of course, not enough is being done in these areas, but when one ignores positive examples, one takes away hope and makes exploitation appear natural and inevitable. It is important to stress I do not want to let my knowledge of some better labor practices make it seem that the problems Childress is addressing do not exist; instead, my goal is to present a more balanced and truthful account that can let people know alternatives are possible.

What is most upsetting about Childress' work is that he dismisses and ignores the labor contingent faculty have been doing for decades. As a result of advocacy by contingent faculty and their allies, not only are some NTT faculty evaluated based on their level of engagement in research and their publishing of scholarly texts, but also some are evaluated for teaching, service, and professional development by their peers, yet Childress makes it seem that all contingent faculty are assessed only by student evaluations and their chair. He states, "For adjuncts, there's even less support for or interest in their research lives, so the only thing that gets reviewed are end-of-semester course evaluations, and those only by the department chair" (106). Once again, this representation denies the reality of the labor of many contingent faculty and feeds into the exploitative logic that NTT faculty only teach and that they have no part in evaluating their colleagues.

To be honest, I do not know whether Childress is simply ignorant of the facts or if his hyperbolic language forces him to reiterate destructive generalizations and prejudices. I would argue that a problem with a certain form of political activism is that it feels that the world has to be represented in stark, extreme terms in order to maximize the emotional appeal to create an argument. The problem with this rhetorical strategy is that it often distorts the truth and can be highly manipulative. Furthermore, while focusing only on the most negative situations can foster a bond through a sense of shared victimization, one might lose any sense of reality or hope that situations can be improved.

Although it is clear that Childress wants to enhance the working conditions of contingent faculty, his mindset blocks him from recognizing all of the different kinds of labor that many of these faculty members are doing on a daily basis. For example, in the following passage, he makes claims not only about NTT faculty but also about TT faculty that are simply too definitive and universal, while the reality is much more complicated and diverse:

> Contingent workers aren't paid to come to meetings, and don't have much time for them anyway, so even those rare schools or departments that open larger discussions to their adjuncts don't get a lot of participation. (Which, of course, can be seen by the TTs as further evidence of adjuncts' lack of interest.) But the larger fact is that even the TT faculty are largely invisible to one another in the details of their daily work. In part because everyone's busy, and in part because of the culture of academic freedom,

> it's extraordinarily uncommon to have one faculty member sitting in on another's classroom; when it does happen, it's usually a chair or a dean exercising oversight, rather than a colleague exercising curiosity about what's going on in those other classes. Teaching is an isolative culture, one that reveres but rarely explores exactly what happens in the sealed box of a classroom. (106)

This passage is filled with overgeneralizations and misrepresentations hiding the labor that many faculty do on a daily basis. Contingent faculty members and TT faculty members have spent countless hours going to meetings and visiting each other's classrooms, and to neglect this reality is to belittle the labor of the people Childress is trying to support. Furthermore, it is strange that he blames academic freedom for contributing to the problems he is discussing. If anything, academic freedom protections often work to make precarious academic labor more sustainable even though many contingent faculty are not protected by this core system of rights and privileges.

Not only does Childress repeat the destructive stereotype that NTT faculty only teach, but he also fails to see the many ways that contingent faculty play a key role in working closely with students. He states,

> if half of the courses are led by impermanent teachers, even the students who fall in love with an adjunct's thinking can never have a second date, can never see a relationship bloom into a new path through the intellectual garden. They might not even be able to see that teacher between classes, as she rushes off to another class session at another school. The possibilities of mentorship are lost when we reduce faculty life to mere instruction. (p. 116)

In his effort to bemoan the way so many contingent faculty are treated, he fails to see that for many undergraduate students, the faculty member they know the best is the one without the possibility for tenure. If this was not true, then many of my colleagues would not be writing so many letters of recommendation. The truth is that most students do not know the employment status of their teachers, so they do not hesitate forming extended relationships with their NTT mentors.

Childress' underlying pessimism and defeatism is made clear in his predictions about the future. He proclaims,

> I think we have likewise passed the point of peak faculty. A combination of consumer thinking, market fluidity, loss of professional status, technological innovation, and demographic shifts has led us to a point where the faculty will never again be a primarily full-time, primarily tenure-track institutional or cultural commitment. There will always be teachers, sure. But the idea of "the faculty" is as dead as the idea of coal; it'll carry on for a while because of sunk costs and the gasping demands of those still left in the industry—but really, it's gone. (135)

The type of rhetoric presented in this passage robs the people he is trying to help of any hope, and much of his pessimism relies on how he is defining the term "faculty." By saying that the faculty are dead, he is indicating that a certain narrow idea of what faculty should be is dying out. On one level, he is correct to point to the reduction of new TT positions, but by overgeneralizing the term "faculty," he dismisses all of the other types of academic labor. Moreover, why should one fight for improvement, if things can only get worse?

Perhaps the most dispiriting aspect of Childress' work comes in his rejection of the ways that unions and other collective actions can improve the plight of contingent faculty. In his opinion,

> We will not eliminate contingency through battles, through unions and collective bargaining, because we can make a school pay people better without respecting them any more fully. We will not eliminate contingency through increased state or federal funding, because we've already demonstrated that there are any number of things to spend money on that are more appealing than a permanent faculty. We will not eliminate contingency through the oversight of accreditors, because we've experienced their willingness to award continued operation to schools that starve the majority of their teachers. (154)

While it is highly likely that contingency might never be completely eliminated, it is wrong to dismiss the way that unions and states have helped to improve the working conditions of many NTT faculty. Furthermore, there are some situations in which contingent positions are desired and necessary. By conflating all faculty into a single definition, Childress simply dismisses the reality of higher education and the value of having different types of faculty positions.

Instead of endorsing collective action and what has worked in the past, Childress' solution revolves around an abstract call to change our values and culture. He exhorts, "We will only eliminate contingency through changing our definitions and our values. We will only eliminate it through cultivating respect, through the decision to reward demonstrated capability and good will rather than roles in an organizational chart" (154–55). This vague idealism pretends to provide a solution, but in fact nothing is really offered; rather, the reality of the material conditions of many precarious workers is denied.

Chapter 5. Tenure for the Contingent?

To gain a deeper insight into the hierarchy of faculty and the role of class consciousness in the divide between TT and NTT faculty, we can look at Michael Bérubé and Jennifer Ruth's book, *The Humanities, Higher Education, and Academic Freedom*, in which they propose granting tenure for all teachers in higher education with Ph.D.s. We shall see that this well-intentioned book unintentionally offers an example of the problematic perspective that many tenured professors hold in relation to their contingent colleagues.

In the third chapter, titled, "From Professionalism to Patronage," the authors begin by providing a long list of the reasons internal to higher education for the growing use of NTT faculty:

> Adjunct hiring has enabled us to do many things we want to do and don't want to give up doing: (1) Hire people with higher courseloads to meet student demand without undertaking the hard work of time-intensive searches. (2) Hire people with higher courseloads without asking whether this should prompt us to build a teaching-intensive tenure track or rethink our conventional jobs bundling teaching, research, and service. (3) Hire spouses not as spousal hires but into non-tenure-track positions since they are easier to secure. (4) Hire people for curricular areas we find alluring without committing to those areas in perpetuity. (5) Grow niche programs on all-adjunct labor to boost our overall student-credit-hour numbers so that we have more capital to ask for tenure lines. (6) Hire adjuncts to give full-time faculty course releases for research and other projects. (7) Add new sections at the last minute when all the others fill up so that our students have the classes they need to graduate. (8) Hire our graduate students in the hope that teaching experience will make them attractive for full-time jobs elsewhere. (9) Continue to run the full gamut of courses during budget crunches that we hope are short-term but that invariably become long-term. Some of these motivations are more understandable than others. All of them have made the world in which we now live. (66–67)

Here we find a focus on the inner dynamics that result in TT faculty unintentionally and intentionally profiting from the exploitation of a lower class of workers who do not have the same compensation or rights. Since it is so easy and efficient to hire NTT faculty at the last minute, tenured professors are incentivized to look the other way as their departments deal with budget cuts and enrollment fluctuations (Nealon). Of course, there is also the need to hire spouses and reduce course loads so professors can focus more on research (Waltman et al.), but as Bérubé and Ruth suggest in this passage, these issues are not being directly confronted.

P&C

In the book, Ruth focuses on a time when she was chair of her program and tried to do the right thing, but she constantly encountered the resistance of the contingent faculty. In the following passage, she articulates her argument that contingent faculty cannot be as focused on the best interests of students as TT faculty because they are always so concerned about losing their jobs:

> Finally, this faculty member blurted, "Look, I am not on the tenure track and all I teach is film. You reduce the film courses students take and I may be out of a job!" The professor in my office asked, "Should we be thinking about our own employment when we decide on curriculum or strictly what we believe to be in the best interests of our students?" Obviously, the latter. We're not here to ensure our own futures but to help students prepare for theirs. Tenured faculty have the ability to make disinterested decisions to this end that other faculty, through no fault of their own, simply don't. This matters in university politics. It matters a lot and it matters often. (74)

The first obvious prejudice re-circulated in this passage is the notion that faculty seeking to protect their own jobs are undermining a concern for students. This argument has been used in the anti-union school choice movement, which often argues that it is tenure that blocks a concern for students. Here, we are told that contingent faculty cannot be as student focused as their tenured colleagues because contingent faculty ultimately only care about keeping their jobs.

To help explain how tenure supposedly turns self-interested people into disinterested professionals, Bérubé and Ruth make the following statement:

> The tenure system acknowledges human nature—namely, the fact that people usually won't act against their own interests, regardless of the larger context. It takes this into account by enabling faculty to deliberate and research and teach and grade without anxiety over the next paycheck warping the outcome of these activities. We don't have to vote on curricular matters to gratify our supervisors, we don't have to deliver lab results that satisfy pharmaceutical companies, we don't have to teach only the subjects our students find entertaining, and we don't have to please them when we submit their grades. (74)

The problem with this passage is that it should be clear that a lot of research done by tenured professors has been shown to be corrupted by the influence of money and the quest for prestige. Also, anyone who has been in a faculty meeting should know that there is rarely an absence of self-interest or an absence of the desire to gratify supervisors. Even full professors want a merit increase or a better teaching schedule or a better parking space. As I have argued throughout this book, if we want faculty members to be more effective, then we have to treat them fairly and justly. For example, by insisting on transparent and objective hiring and review practices, we can enhance workplace democracy for everyone.

Instead of directly confronting the real level of exploitation and prejudice in the academic labor system, the authors suggest the following:

> TT faculty, at least at poorly funded state schools like mine, tend not to see themselves as the worthy elite but as the downtrodden. This may come as a surprise to a public traumatized by the recession. Certainly, adjunct instructors might assume that TT faculty salaries, benefits, job security, and empowerment in shared governance would preclude this group from identifying with the Joads. (81)

While it may be true that a group of faculty at a non-elite institution identify themselves as the victims of the system, this does not mean that there is not an even greater class of exploited workers in academia. Moreover, after presenting a discourse of comparative victimhood, Bérubé and Ruth make the following argument:

> Telling these [tenured] faculty members they should identify as labor is telling them something they like hearing. It reinforces their sense that they are overworked and underappreciated. It also acts as a kind of Get-out-of-Jail-Free card with regard to whatever guilt they may feel about the genuinely downtrodden in their midst. In short, and at the risk of sounding cynical, we are in danger of embracing the identity of labor so that we absolve ourselves of responsibility for having poorly managed our affairs and generated our own underclass. (82)

According to this logic, telling professors that they should identify with labor and organize with labor unions will only have the result of making the faculty feel less guilty about their relative privileged status. Despite what Bérubé and Ruth claim, the reality is that many faculty do not want to identify themselves as workers or be unionized because they like to see themselves as elite professionals.

The reverse side of this disidentification by tenured faculty is the claim that when contingent faculty do identify with their exploited status, they only end up showing how they are reliant on the kindness of individual administrators for their jobs, even in the context of unionized faculty. Bérubé and Ruth state, "Indeed, when contingent faculty call themselves the serfs, peasants, or helots of academe, they drive home a real point–that their initial and then continued existence at an institution is contingent on the pleasure of individuals with tenure, even when they are represented by a faculty union" (99). I believe the authors have this exactly backwards. For instance, the UC-AFT union has used the collective bargaining process and other forms of due process to try to stop the practice of basing academic decisions on individual favors and prejudices.

These professors also argue that the use of NTT faculty undermines shared governance and academic freedom because contingent faculty care only about protecting their own positions:

> Furthermore, as I mentioned earlier, NTT involvement in governance can accelerate the erosion of tenure. Here's how it has done so in my

department: (1) NTT involvement has made it virtually impossible to handle budget cuts in any way other than by canceling job searches that were replacements for retiring tenure-line faculty. Who would choose to not rehire someone with whom you have been involved in all kinds of departmental and university discussions and deliberations? So when a budget "crisis" erupts (which happens every year at my university, typically after we've received approval to replace retired tenured faculty but before we've begun a search), we cancel a search. It is much easier to cut a position to be held by some hypothetical future colleague than to cut a position held by someone you see on a regular basis. Over time, this means fewer tenure lines and more NTT lines. (2) NTT involvement creates various conflicts of interest, as it did in my department. Even discussing what areas in which to hire after someone has retired becomes complicated when an NTT faculty member has begun filling in by teaching this or that related subject. She may not have a terminal degree or expertise in the area but she, and the people who worry about her, may feel that her job will become more insecure if we hire people in certain areas. (92)

I find this passage to be a rationalization for denying shared governance rights to the majority of the faculty. First of all, it is simply wrong to say that NTT faculty are always rehired because no one wants to hurt the feelings of a colleague. The reality is that many contingent faculty are defined by the ease of replacing them. Furthermore, just because it is easier emotionally to retain a contingent faculty member during a budget crisis than to eliminate that position in order to retain a tenure line does not mean that NTT positions undermine tenure. Instead, as I have been arguing, secure NTT faculty jobs help to provide a middle ground between tenure and pure contingency. However, this liminal space is ignored by the binary logic of many tenured professors such as Bérubé and Ruth.

The next argument the authors make flies in the face of my experience teaching in two programs where almost all of the faculty running the program were off of the tenure track. They claim,

Academic committee work may be easily ridiculed as a professorial version of Dilbert, but it actually consists of professors articulating and negotiating the terms of their employment, their expertise, their research projects, their course assignments, and their engagements with students. What results from these negotiations cannot be chalked up to hierarchy; it is the outcome of genuinely shared governance. "Shared," here, does not mean that the negotiations are without heat and conflict, of course. What it does mean is that nobody has recourse to an outside authority other than reality (think budgets not bosses) to resolve the conflicts that arise. This lends the discussions their (sometimes) exhilarating air of spontaneity and authenticity. Spontaneity and candor are destroyed and different concerns move to the fore. The orientation of

> the room shifts almost palpably from a focus on the needs of the students, the institution, or the discipline to a focus on the needs of the faculty themselves. (112)

This passage is structured by a set of prejudices and stereotypes that ends up blaming the victims of labor exploitation instead of affirming that by denying contingent faculty academic freedom or shared governance rights or job stability, democracy for all faculty is underminded.

One possible reason for this discourse of blaming the victim is that often even the most supportive and progressive tenured professors do not want to admit their roles in the exploitation of their colleagues. It can be much more comforting to blame evil administrators or neoliberalism for the casualization of the academic labor force. However, as I argued in Chapter 1, the origins of the deprofessionalization of the faculty in part can be traced to the way many faculty in the sciences were motivated by governmental funds after World War II to focus on their research as a source of prestige and enhanced compensation. Since the faculty members who gained funding to increase their research activities needed people to teach their courses, they turned to graduate students and part-time faculty. None of this was well planned, but the result was that the professional status of professors was hollowed out from the inside. When faculty began focusing on their research and individual careers, a space was left open for administrators to take over many of the tasks that were once handled by TT faculty. In other words, the restructuring of the professoriate did not happen solely due to the external corporatization of the university; instead, internal actors were incentivized to focus their efforts on their research and individual careers. Although the policies and economics of neoliberalism have contributed to the downsizing of the faculty and the casualization of the labor force, it would be wrong to focus only on these external forces.

In the case of Bérubé and Ruth's text, we see many of the reasons why people do not like the new liberal professional class. A mode of smug self-idealization is coupled with a debasement of people who do not fit into the same class. In what Thomas Frank has called meritocratic narcissism, we see how some of the tenured elites buy into the myths surrounding their own excellence as they discount the suffering of the working class. This is similar to one reason why some have argued the Democrats have lost power, by giving up on focusing on organized labor and the working class and instead becoming the party of the professional elite (Frank).

In order to form a more progressive politics inside and outside of higher education, it is necessary to bridge the divide between workers and professional elites. As we are seeing in so many different areas of human labor, automation is making every job vulnerable, so it is in everyone's best interest to push for better job protections for all workers. The next chapter will seek to outline some ways contingent faculty can work together to overcome the creation of the new gig academy.

Chapter 6. Conclusion: Fighting for a Democratic Workplace at the Gig Academy

To conclude this book, I want to examine what my analysis of precarious faculty working conditions and organizing can tell us about the broader labor market and employment structure in higher education. In fact, what most people do not know is that higher education has been one of the greatest producers of new models of labor exploitation. From unpaid internships to undergraduate peer teachers, universities and colleges never seem to tire of creating different ways to get workers to do their jobs with little or no compensation. My argument is that since these institutions have helped to create the current predicament, they may also help us to envision a different future. As I have argued throughout this book, one key element for positive social change is employees who demand more workplace democracy.

The Real Roots of the Gig Academy

In Kezar et al.'s *The Gig Academy*, we see how the casualization of the labor force has moved to all areas of the academic economy. The key components of the new employment structure include "a fissured and misclassified workforce; unbundled, deprofessionalized, and atomized roles; forced micro-entrepreneurship; managerial influence over labor supply and demand; offloading costs onto workers; technological means of reducing labor costs; and increasing structural discrimination" (20). I have been arguing that we can trace many of these changes in how workers are treated to the ways universities turned to a casualized labor force after World War II. If we want to understand the roots of our current employment structures, we have to look at how liberal, middle-class professionals responded to government-sponsored incentives by turning themselves into careerist entrepreneurs (Hedges). My argument is that the original cause behind the gig academy was not just the development of external neoliberal policies in the 1970s; rather, these transforming employment practices were partially developed out of an internal restructuring of labor relations starting in the 1950s.

The reason why I believe it is so important to understand the roots of the casualization of the academic labor force and the broader economy is that if one wants to fix current problems, one has to see that we cannot simply blame neoliberal ideology, state defunding, technological transformations, or a corporate administrative takeover. All of these key aspects of our contemporary gig economy were made possible in part by liberal middle-class professionals trading in their shared public missions for a focus on individual careers, prestige, and profits (Ehrenreich 5–6).

One of the main ways that professors during the Cold War helped to usher in the gig academy was by unintentionally splitting off teaching and service from research (Nisbet). In other words, they unbundled their own profession by concentrating their efforts and attention on the competition for government-funded research. In *The Gig Academy*, Kezar and her colleagues offer a different framing narrative:

> … unbundling is a crucial arrow in the quiver of Gig Academy managers. This trend developed directly out of the discourse on "scientific management," also known by the moniker "Taylorism," after its creator. The key is to study complex work processes and devise ways to reproduce them by disassembling the tacit expertise of highly skilled workers into the simplest components. Each of these components is standardized in order to distill the process down to a mechanical sequence that can be delivered far more cheaply by substituting or supplementing low- to middle-skilled labor. In this manner, the contemporary university has managed to break down complicated professional roles like those of academic faculty, which paved the way to displace large portions of work onto contingent hires. (23)

This common way of seeing the causes of the unbundling of the professions blames top-down managers for imposing a discourse of scientific management, yet I have been arguing that in the case of research universities, the picture is much more complicated because it was the faculty themselves who unintentionally spun off their roles in teaching and administration. From this perspective, the protections of tenure were not used to protect a public good; instead, tenured professors were able to use their academic freedom and autonomy to pursue their own careers. Thus, tenure was perverted from the inside as faculty willingly restructured their own jobs and moved from a collective mission to a more individualistic understanding of academic work.[10]

It is therefore not very surprising that professors like Bérubé and Ruth reveal a distrust in the ability of NTT faculty to act in a collective manner, even though the truth is that tenured professors themselves have often been trained to be self-interested careerists who rely on the labor of others to focus on their own prestige and compensation. My goal here is not to deny the importance of contingent faculty working with tenured professors to build a more democratic and just workplace; rather, I want to argue that we need to begin with a frank assessment of the origins and effects of our current labor system. After all, if we simply blame the state or neoliberal ideology rather than addressing the class conflicts inherent to universities and colleges themselves, we will not be able to make important improvements. For instance, in the current labor structure

---

10. For a discussion of the pros and cons of individualism vs. collaboration in the tenure and promotion process, see Kemp.

at research universities, tenured professors often rely on graduate students to take their graduate seminars, teach their undergraduate courses, and work in their scientific labs (Bousquet, "The Waste Product"). These professors are then structurally reliant on a class of exploited workers in order to maintain their own class positions. Moreover, since the same universities that produce Ph.D.s also hire these credentialed students off of the tenure track (Bousquet, "Introduction" 1–2), the institutions are creating their own source of surplus labor to be exploited. While I do not think that much of this structure is intentional, what has been created is a system where professors are incentivized to turn a blind eye to their own role in deprofessionalizing their profession, a process similar to one described by Nina Toren as having happened in relation to other professions.

Since some research professors in the sciences are so busy doing their research and competing for funding, they may not only step away from instruction but also administration (Washburn). Furthermore, research projects require a great deal of staffing and oversight, so they contribute to administrative bloat (Newfield). While federal and state grants often include a certain amount of funding for staff and other forms of overhead, it is unclear whether research usually pays for itself. In fact, there is a lot of evidence pointing to the fact that undergraduate instruction often subsidizes research, and one reason why institutions have to rely on exploited contingent and graduate student labor is that they have to generate a "profit" to pay for expensive research projects (Samuels, *Why Public Higher Education*).

As I mentioned in the introduction of this book and as I address in *The Politics of Writing Studies*, the Cold War funding system helped to create a structure containing several related hierarchies: research over teaching; the sciences over the humanities; theory over practice; graduate education over undergraduate education; professors over contingent faculty; and careerism over public mission (10–11). By responding to specific incentives, science professors were able to restructure higher education from the inside in an unintentional fashion, and while it is true that only a small percentage of higher education institutions are designated as Research I schools, these universities train and influence faculty from a wide range of institutions. One of the main ways the Cold War science professors helped to transform the faculty was through their focus on their individual careers. Even though many of these faculty members were participating in the national effort to defend the United States against perceived threats coming from the Soviet Union and other communist states, the fight for funding and prestige created a type of individualistic ethos:

> Individualism can serve as an ethic that disrupts the collective consciousness necessary for questioning and disrupting unequal power conditions. With the breakdown of community also comes many other problematic outcomes, including disengagement, poor morale, and alienation, that are hindering higher education in meeting its outcomes and being effective. (Schmit 6)

Here we see how a careerist mentality focused on individual rewards and prestige can undermine the ability to make the workplace more fair and just. Furthermore, since many professors do not have a collective understanding of their own profession, they may ignore the poor working conditions of their fellow workers. Not only does this system make contingent teachers feel disempowered and alienated, but it can also lead to the disaffection of the research professors themselves. My goal here is not to demonize research professors in the sciences; rather, I want to show how since the root causes of the academic gig economy have to be traced back to the actions of the liberal academic professional class, the solutions will have to take into account this constituency and ideology.

● Tenured Allies?

One way that I have seen TT and NTT faculty work together is by focusing on projects of shared interest, such as addressing the increase in administrative costs and the reduction of state funding for higher education. Although some professors may not want to confront the exploitation of contingent labor, they might be willing to enter into a shared alliance with contingent faculty over other issues. My experience has been that once TT and NTT faculty start to address issues together, they start to build relationships that can lead to a raising of consciousness concerning labor conditions.

An example that I have witnessed of TT and NTT faculty working together was the fight over online education in California. After the Great Recession, many higher education administrators and state officials believed the best way to increase graduation rates and reduce spending was to turn to massive online courses (Vardi 5). The UC system union worked with other unions and different faculty groups to fight this change because it knew that it would probably increase costs and eliminate many faculty jobs. In partnering with faculty senates, the union was able to use research concerning online education to resist the changes that were being promoted from above. During this process, the union built lasting relationships across faculty lines, relationships that were later used to fight the attempted restructuring of pensions. One thing the union learned from these joint ventures is that working with people holding different faculty positions helped to build a more collective mindset that could later be used to address issues concerning working conditions and labor exploitation. However, the recent turn to online education due to the COVID-19 pandemic reveals how the good work accomplished by the alliance between TT and NTT faculty was easily undone in a state of emergency where almost everyone relinquished power to administrative control.

The move to remote education through administrative fiat is just one example of how a growing administrative class, as documented by Jay Greene and his colleagues (14), can result in a more powerful administration. Additionally, TT professors have ceded power as they have focused on their research careers at the expense of service in the shape of administrative duties. As a result, professors now feel disempowered, as noted by Kezar et al. in *The Gig Academy*:

> Power is a pervasive theme. Faculty and staff have lost power, and administrators are centralizing and gaining power. Postdocs and graduate students are asserting power as they find themselves as laborers. We argue that the consolidation of power among administrators does not serve higher education institutions. Our ultimate recommendations are centered around workplace democracy that is based on notions of power redistribution to ameliorate existing labor problems. (7)

The question we must ask about this situation is, did faculty give up their power or was it taken from them? I have been arguing that in many cases, the administrative power was taken from them because they gave it up by focusing on other areas of their jobs.

In response to this labor dynamic, those of us working in higher education have witnessed during the last couple of decades a revolution from below as the most disempowered faculty and staff workers have tried to organize and resist what they see as the corporate administrative takeover of their institutions, but this process is bound to fail if it does not also address the structural hierarchies that support the dominance of the liberal professional academic class. The problem I have with simply blaming the restructuring of higher education on neoliberal ideology is that it fails to address the role played by liberal professionals in creating many of the conditions and structures that made neoliberalism possible. For instance, in their discussion of neoliberalism in *The Gig Academy*, Kezar and her co-authors focus on the post 1980s political ideology of the Right, stating, "General neoliberal tendencies include prioritizing individual freedoms over collective liberty and personal responsibility over shared welfare. They also include a preference for shifting responsibility over the provision of basic needs and public goods from democratic institutions to private enterprises" (14). The counter-narrative I have presented argues that this shift from liberal democratic institutions and policies to a right-wing vision of free market determinism was actually initiated by liberal middle-class professionals. Ironically, public institutions of higher education were transformed into quasi-private enterprises through a form of Cold War welfare for scientific research (Lowen). However, instead of seeing this transformation as merely the imposition of a government-based funding model, it is vital to look at how liberal professionals responded to new funding incentives by restructuring their own jobs in an effort to chase prestige and enhanced compensation. From this perspective, those of us working in higher education will never make its labor system just and fair if we do not confront the institutional hierarchies that were mainly generated from within.

One possible solution would be for the federal government to tie research funding to the fair treatment of all employees associated with the research. In fact, research grants already impose several strict requirements regarding spending and budgeting (Noll and Rogerson 5), so it should be possible to force institutions that receive federal support for research to rely on non-exploited labor. Likewise, Pell grants and other forms of federal financial aid could require that institutions with students who receive such aid have minimum standards for pay and job security. Additionally, state governments can play a role. Since teachers at public institutions of higher education are state employees, states can require fair working conditions for all faculty. While some movement has occurred in certain states to legislate protections for contingent faculty, there is much work that can be done (Schneirov). It is worth noting that since more workers in the overall workforce are participating in the gig economy, legislatures are being forced to rethink employment law and state policies regarding precarious labor (Lobel).

● We're All Contingent Now

As Kezar and her fellow authors stress in *The Gig Academy*, the entire economy is turning to the casualization of the labor force,

> ... the contingent workforce has increased by more than 50 percent ... rising from 10.7 percent of the total workforce in 1995 to 15.8 percent in 2015. ... Intuit, owner of TurboTax software, recently estimated that more than double that percentage work contingently, based on an analysis of the data it has from 2016 tax filings. Perhaps more ominously, researchers found that expansion of this labor segment accounts for around 95 percent of the net growth in employment in the two decades since 1995. (16–17).

This move to precarious labor in the general economy means that the issues facing contingent faculty in higher education are evident in many other professions. Likewise, many of the solutions we have seen regarding improving the working conditions of contingent faculty can also be applied to issues concerning workers outside of higher education. For example, all workers need a fair and transparent hiring and promotion process. They also need to be compensated for all of their work, and the government has to guard against the misclassification and the proliferation of new exploited classes of workers (De Stefano). Moreover, as I showed in my discussion of the UC system contract, employees should be given support for professional development, and they need a say in how their work is defined and assessed.

Those of us working in higher education can use knowledge we have gained from working to improve the labor conditions of contingent faculty to help other precarious workers by demonstrating the power of collective organizing and coalition building. Too many gig workers see themselves as isolated, independent contractors without any rights or benefits. Luckily, in California, a bill was passed that prevents companies from hiring people as "independent contractors"; instead, they must be treated as regular employees, which gives them full protection under the law (Semuels). Changing independent contractors to regular employees helps eliminate job misclassification. As Kezar and her colleagues highlight in *The Gig Academy*, the problem of job misclassification has many side effects:

> These misclassifications matter, particularly to workers on the receiving end, who lose basic protections of employment, including minimum wage and overtime protection, as well as social safety net protections, such as workers' compensation and unemployment insurance, because independent contractors do not contribute to those funds. But they also matter to the polity, since misclassified workers can be used to craft exemptions from payroll taxes, which would otherwise cycle back into the public coffers. (22)

This use of misclassification, or the wrong job title, is very common in higher education and may be an innovation that has spread throughout the labor market (Bensman 7–10). In other words, while many people see universities and colleges as liberal institutions, these organization have led the way in producing new ways of exploiting workers. Not only do universities rely on producing their own surplus labor, but through their creation of internships and student employee positions, they have helped to develop ways to hide labor exploitation (Braun 281–287).

Universities also rely on convincing workers that because they are pursuing a higher calling, they do not need to be treated fairly, and this ideology has now spread to the general gig economy. Kezar and her co-authors of *The Gig Academy* explain how this reasoning works, writing, "Gig work conjures the image of the artist and bohemian, who seeks to remain untethered and therefore free to pursue activities of passion–a freedom which may be culturally signaled at least in part by a rebellious indifference to long-term planning for financial security" (24). This combination of artistic and academic values can be seen best in the use and abuse of graduate student instructors who are socialized to see their labor exploitation as a way of developing their career as they pursue their creative interests; however, not only are these students exploited as graduate workers, but some will later be exploited as contingent faculty, and in many ways, their graduate education helps to normalize for them their future precarious labor.

Fixing the use and abuse of graduate student instructors is therefore a key part of transforming the working conditions of contingent faculty because these workers are not only exploited while they are students but also often conditioned to accept such working conditions later when they are teachers. Furthermore, the trend of having students pursue post-doctorate fellowships prior to being hired in TT faculty positions adds another level of potential labor exploitation, as post-docs often are poorly paid, receive little or no benefits, and do not have long-term contracts (Stephan 245). At this point, we have to ask why do so many liberals and liberal institutions participate in this process of the deprofessionalization and casualization of the higher education labor force? I believe that one answer to this question involves the unconscious psychology of liberal people, which involves the need to be seen by the self and others as being moral and good; since liberals desire to have their good self recognized by others, any bad actions or bad effects have to be repressed or denied (Samuels, "(Liberal) Narcissism"). Thus, liberal professors may fail to see that they are exploiting their graduate students because they do not want to believe that their good intentions can lead to bad effects. Moreover, the desire to blame the problems of higher education on evil administrators and state budget cuts may serve to shield liberal professors from seeing their own role in a destructive system.

Perhaps the ultimate contradiction of these liberal institutions is that they are often obsessed by the conflicting missions of equality and prestige. Liberals want to believe that their institutions support the goals of building a more just and equal society, but they also want to be recognized for their high status (Samuels, *Educating Inequality*). In fact, the conflicting desires for equal opportunity and recognized talent embodies the idea of a meritocracy, and in the structure of higher education, professors striving for increased prestige and compensation often hide behind the belief that they are contributing to the common good by promoting a meritocracy (McNamee and Miller). This self-deception, then, blinds many liberals from seeing the labor exploitation that makes their lives possible.

● Rate Your Employee

Not only do liberal professors often turn a blind eye to the workers around them, but also they have instituted and maintained a system of faculty evaluations based on student feedback that has been shown to be highly biased and discriminatory (Scherr and Scherr). Similarly, as Kezar and her colleagues reveal in *The Gig Academy*, the use of customer ratings in the general gig economy is problematic:

> But as Hannák et al. recently uncovered in their study of bias in app-based freelance work, women and people of color face significant job discrimination, as structural social biases also get aggregated in the form of negative customer feedback and lower ratings, which ultimately reduces their earnings. Worse, these services often enforce minimum rating standards, meaning workers can find themselves permanently banned from the platform at a moment's notice and without recourse if they fail to meet the minimum level of customer satisfaction, undoubtedly a fate more likely to befall those who already experience arbitrary social bias. (31)

It is interesting to think about the ways the use of student evaluations in higher education is similar to customer ratings in the gig economy. In both cases, employers outsource their role in assessing the effectiveness of their workers, and both systems rely on using unqualified evaluators to make judgments based on bias and personal reactions. It's also interesting to note that the problematic anonymity of student evaluations seems similar to the sometimes problematic use of anonymity in online discussions and comment sections, the latter of which is discussed by Hiroaki Morio and Christopher Buchholz. Here we see how universities and colleges have not only been innovators in practices that undermine workers, such as through the use of anonymous student evaluations of faculty, but also innovators in technologies that harm social equality by allowing anonymity in discussion forums. Yet, since we believe that these liberal institutions are shaped by good intentions, we often deny their role in destructive social practices.

The fact that universities and colleges continue to use student evaluations after they have been proven to be unscientific and biased points to the failure of liberalism to protect workers against discrimination and exploitation. As Kezar and her co-authors relate in *The Gig Academy*, student evaluations are a troubling application of free market principles:

> In a 2015 interview with the *Chronicle of Higher Education*, the founder of Udemy (a prominent MOOC platform) argues that student ratings are the ideal form of instructional quality control: "In an open marketplace where there is competition, if you're an instructor and you can't teach well or you don't know what you're talking about, students will say so with ratings . . . *If you're not providing value, you won't make money*—only the best teachers go to the top." The most obvious problem with this statement is that there is a great deal of empirical evidence to show that student evaluations of teaching are not always measures of instructional quality, and they show clear bias on the basis of race, gender, and perceived political orientation. (31–32)

Not only does the practice of student evaluations as described in this passage transform the assessment of teaching by qualified professionals into a popularity contest fueled by biased students, but this invention is coupled with de-professionalization through the celebration of the amateur; since any student is seen as qualified to judge professional experts, expertise no longer matters, and, as Peter Sacks explains, the student is positioned to be the customer of a provided educational service (xiii).

Once again, it is important to stress that student evaluations were not imposed by interfering states or corporatized neoliberal administrators but were instituted by the liberal faculty themselves (Trout). Of course, many research professors do not have to worry about these evaluations because they are promoted primarily for their research, grants, and publications rather than for their teaching, but for NTT faculty, these faulty tools are often used to form the basis of decisions about teaching assignments or even firings (Heller A8). Any talk about having a diverse faculty and promoting a more equal society is undermined by the use of assessment tools that have been shown to be highly biased. In fact, when the UC-AFT union tried to bargain over the elimination of student evaluations, it was told that no one wanted to spend the time and resources on a different method. Fortunately, there is a growing movement calling these evaluations into question. Once again, a change may occur because people first organized from below, and then later, people with more power took on the fight.

● Hiring Fairly

Coupled with this question concerning how contingent faculty are assessed is the issue of how they are hired and how they are let go. As I documented in Chapter 2, the UC-AFT contract requires schools to provide a clear career path with specific guidelines concerning under what conditions a lecturer can be let go and what type of warning is necessary for a layoff. However, there are still many faculty in their first six years who are simply not rehired for no stated reason. Since precarious positions exist in part to give management flexibility in the face of fluctuating enrollments, it is hard to see how to fix some of these problems, yet, due to the threat of lawsuits concerning discriminatory workplace practices as described by Susan Bisom-Rapp (970), many campuses have started to require national searches for all positions, and these searches have to follow strict guidelines. We have found that one effect of this administrative change is that institutions are forced to make a much stronger commitment to contingent faculty in order to attract viable candidates.

A key in stabilizing these positions is to make sure that all faculty are hired through a clear and rigorous process so that the positions become more regularized and predictable. Unfortunately, as Kezar and her co-authors explain in *The Gig Academy*, fair hiring and dismissal practices for contingent faculty in higher education are the exception and not the norm:

> With little or no job security they are typically hired semester-to-semester or year-to-year, often within weeks or days of the semester's beginning, so they have very little ability to predict their work schedules, obligations, and even income. In fact, a study by the Center for the Future of Higher Education found last-minute hiring to be rampant, with more than a third of contingent instructors reporting they were hired within just three weeks of the start of classes and more than a sixth within two weeks. (43)

It should be clear that these common hiring practices expose institutions to the potential for lawsuits regarding discriminatory practices.

One of the major pushes the UC-AFT union and other unions and professional organizations around the country have undertaken is to motivate institutions to hire their faculty on a full-time basis. Not only do full-time faculty have more stable careers, but they can spend more time with students because they do not have to run between jobs at different schools. In many cases, fringe benefits kick in once someone has at least a 50 percent appointment, so it does not cost more to have one full-time position instead of two half-time positions, and money can be saved by cutting down on the cost of hiring and training so many part-time faculty. FTNTT positions offer a middle ground between pure contingency and tenure, and although some may see these positions as representing an erosion of the tenure system, these positions may be an effective compromise balancing institutional and employee needs.

By creating a career path for contingent faculty, academic institutions can not only stabilize their workforce, but they can also help to make these jobs functional by providing raises and promotions based on clear and fair assessment practices (Schwartz). This emphasis on creating stable, full-time positions clearly goes against many of the current practices that Kezar and her colleagues describe in *The Gig Academy*: "Part-time faculty typically lack any promotional opportunities or bridges to secure employment. This means they have little recourse to substantially grow their salary or earn rewards for good performance" (46). To counter this system of casualized labor, faculty need to work together to change the policies and practices at their institutions. A way to enact some of these changes is to seek to rewrite the faculty handbook or notify human resources about potential lawsuits stemming from discriminatory hiring practices.

● Privatizing the Public

One of the central arguments of Kezar and her fellow authors in *The Gig Academy* is that the underlying force reshaping higher education and other professions is the role played by an anti-social mode of capitalistic individualism: "Academic capitalism leaves behind notions of a public or collective good, worker empowerment and participation in decision-making, community among workers, unions and organizing among workers, and public-sector employment relationships, and instead privileges a radical individualism and the privatization of institutional operations" (77). As I have argued, the root causes of this privatization of higher education can be traced to the way that individual professors in the sciences were incentivized to focus on their own careers and not their institutions or their students. One problem with injecting such a market-based system into a social institution is that people may choose to focus on their own desires for more power, prestige, and profit while they eliminate the social and collective spirit of the institution's mission. While some professors did agree to join unions, many professors helped to create an ideology of free agency, which broke the bonds they had to the larger academic community.

One thing I want to stress is that the type of contingent positions I have been documenting throughout this book represent a middle ground between the professional liberal class of the TT faculty and the working class of the adjunct faculty. The kind of FTNTT employment I have been calling for also calls into question many of the binary oppositions that structure higher education hierarchies. This is because FTNTT positions represent a liminal space between teaching and research, careerism and public mission, and at-will hires and tenured security. Moreover, when people who hold such jobs are represented by a union or some other collective organization, the unions can help to counter the tendency to pit each contingent worker against the other. In fact, as Kezar and her co-authors explain in *The Gig Academy*, a defining aspect of the gig academy is the replacement of group solidarity with an ethos of competitive individualism:

> Individualism is achieved by promulgating values of entrepreneurialism so that people see themselves as solely responsible for areas of educational work and as competing with others. Privatization is achieved through market-based values that defund public higher education and encourage a competition for scarce resources, which also reinforces individualism. Inherent in the individualistic logic and the privatizing logic is a move away from collective or community values for organizing higher education. (77)

One way to counter this privatization and individualization of higher education is through the collective organizing of workers from below. Since contingent faculty are often forced to enter a desperate competition for scarce employment, they are pushed into a hyper-competitive market system, but when they become part of a union or professional organization, they have the opportunity to work together on a shared mission of democratizing education.

In states where unions are allowed, teachers can go on strike, which happened with the K-12 teachers in Chicago in 2012, for example (Uetricht 2). However, even when states do not allow contingent faculty to be represented by unions and collective bargaining agreements, teachers can still increase their power and their sense of democratic solidarity, and they will likely find support in their local communities:

> In many states such as Tennessee, West Virginia, Arizona, and Oklahoma—all "right-to-work" states—there are very few labor protections in place. For public-sector workers, striking is a crime. Yet despite the aggressive efforts of many conservative lawmakers and commentators to demonize those who recently participated in statewide teachers strikes as prioritizing their own enrichment over students, communities in these states overwhelmingly sided with their children's teachers, largely due to being well organized. (Kezar et al. 155)

Although unions often provide the best path for protecting the working conditions of precarious faculty, within the current political climate, it is sometimes necessary to take collective action outside of the collective bargaining process. As we have seen, sometimes this means a group of faculty join together and write a petition or show up uninvited to a departmental meetings; the important thing is that precarious workers band together so that they do not accept being reduced to acting as isolated individuals competing for scarce resources.

● Fighting for a Democratic Workplace

In countries such as Germany, with its federal work life programs, when workers are given a greater voice in decision making, workplaces not only become more productive, but the programs also function to protect workers against unemployment and under-employment, and within this structure, workers sit on the boards of most corporations, and they are given the rights of democratic participation in all levels of their employment (Fricke). For Americans, the idea of a democratic workplace sounds absurd; yet, it occurs in many different places throughout the world (Pausch 16).

On reason why American workplaces are not more just is that we do not even think it is possible to have a democratic working environment. However, a growing body of international research has demonstrated the viability and need for workers to play an increased role in decision-making in all aspects of their occupations. Since we live in a democratic society, the same principles of equal citizenship should be applied to the institutions in which we spend our working lives. As Robert Mayer explains, from the perspective of Robert Dahl, it makes no sense to have a democratic political order but a largely authoritarian workplace (222).

As I have argued in this book, progress for improving the working conditions of precarious workers often occurs through the accumulation of small collective acts that build on each other and create a space for the formation of collective coalitions. Part of this process requires overcoming the stereotypes and prejudices that reinforce institutional hierarchies. It is also vital to recognize where improvements have been implemented so that people have hope in an enhanced way of doing things. By learning about examples of better practices and policies for contingent faculty, we can think about how to improve the working conditions of all people laboring in our contemporary economic order.

P&C

Works Cited

Alinsky, Saul D. *Reveille for Radicals*. Vintage Books, 1989.

Auxter, Thomas. "Organizing Faculty Unions in a Right-to-Work Environment." *Journal of Collective Bargaining in the Academy*, vol. 8, no. 1, Dec. 2016, https://thekeep.eiu.edu/jcba/vol8/iss1/8/.

Bensman, David. "Misclassification: Workers in the Borderland." *Journal of Self-Governance and Management Economics*, vol. 2, no. 2, 2014, pp. 7–25.

Berry, Joe. *Reclaiming the Ivory Tower: Organizing Adjuncts to Change Higher Education*. Monthly Review Press, 2005.

Bérubé, Michael, and Jennifer Ruth. *The Humanities, Higher Education, and Academic Freedom: Three Necessary Arguments*. Palgrave Macmillan, 2015. *Springer Link*, https://doi.org/10.1057/9781137506122.

Besosa, Mayra, et al. "Conversion of Appointments to the Tenure Track." *Academe*, vol. 95, no. 6, Nov.-Dec. 2009, pp. 89–99. *JSTOR*, https://www.jstor.org/stable/20694598.

Betensky, Carolyn. "'Tenured Allies' and the Normalization of Contingent Labor." *Academe*, vol. 103, no. 5, Sept.-Oct. 2017, https://www.aaup.org/article/tenured-allies-and-normalization-contingent-labor.

Bisom-Rapp, Susan. "Bulletproofing the Workplace: Symbol and Substance in Employment Discrimination Law Practice." *Florida State University Law Review*, vol. 26, no. 4, summer 1999, pp. 959–1049, https://ir.law.fsu.edu/lr/vol26/iss4/7.

Blackmore, Paul, and Camille B. Kandiko. "Motivation in Academic Life: A Prestige Economy." *Research in Post-Compulsory Education*, vol. 16, no. 4, 2011, pp. 399–411, https://doi.org/10.1080/13596748.2011.626971.

Blankenship, Chris, and Justin M. Jory. "Non-Tenure Track Activism: Genre Appropriation in Program Reporting." *Contingency, Exploitation, and Solidarity: Labor and Action in English Composition*, edited by Seth Kahn et al., The WAC Clearinghouse, UP of Colorado, 2017, pp. 151–67, https://doi.org/10.37514/PER-B.2017.0858.2.10.

Boldt, Joshua A. "An Adjunct Collaborative: Economic Agency and the Professorial Subaltern." *Transformations: The Journal of Inclusive Scholarship and Pedagogy*, vol. 23, no. 1, spring/summer 2012, pp. 95–101. *JSTOR*, https://www.jstor.org/stable/10.5325/trajincschped.23.1.0095.

Bousquet, Marc. *How the University Works: Higher Education and the Low-Wage Nation*. New York UP, 2008.

——. "Introduction: Does a 'Good Job Market in Composition' Help Composition Labor?" *Tenured Bosses and Disposable Teachers: Writing Instruction in the Managed University*, edited by Bousquet at al., Southern Illinois UP, 2004, pp. 1–10.

——. "The Waste Product of Graduate Education: Toward a Dictatorship of the Flexible." *Social Text*, vol. 20, no. 1, spring 2002, pp. 81–104, https://doi.org/10.1215/01642472-20-1_70-81.

Brasket, Deborah J. "Independence and Coalition Building in California: Part-Time Faculty Organize Statewide to End the Exploitation." *Forum: Newsletter of the Non-Tenure-Track Faculty Interest Group*, vol. 3, no. 2, spring 2000, pp. A9-A12, https://prod-ncte-cdn.azureedge.net/nctefiles/groups/cccc/forum/forum0302.pdf.

Braun, Sarah. "The Obama Crackdown: Another Failed Attempt to Regulate the Exploitation of Unpaid Internships." *Southwestern Law Review*, vol. 41, 2011, pp. 281–297.

Brill, Harry. "False Promises of Higher Education: More Graduates, Fewer Jobs." *Against the Current*, no. 82, Sept./Oct. 1999, https://againstthecurrent.org/atc082/p1706/.

Bronfenbrenner, Kate, et al., eds. *Organizing to Win: New Research on Union Strategies.* ILR Press, 1998.

Buller, Jeffrey L. *Best Practices in Faculty Evaluation: A Practical Guide for Academic Leaders.* Jossey-Bass, 2012.

Butler, Judith, et al. *Contingency, Hegemony, Universality: Contemporary Dialogues on the Left.* Verso, 2000.

Carter, Shannon, et al. "Introduction: What Does Democracy Look Like?" *Writing Democracy: The Political Turn in and Beyond the Trump Era*, edited by Carter et al., Routledge, 2020, pp. 1–24.

Childress, Herb. *The Adjunct Underclass: How America's Colleges Betrayed Their Faculty, Their Students, and Their Mission.* U of Chicago P, 2019.

Colby, Richard, and Rebekah Shultz Colby. "Real Faculty But Not: The Full-Time, Non-Tenure-Track Position as Contingent Labor." *Contingency, Exploitation, and Solidarity: Labor and Action in English Composition*, edited by Seth Kahn et al., The WAC Clearinghouse, UP of Colorado, 2017, pp. 57–7, https://doi.org/10.37514/PER-B.2017.0858.2.04.

Cole, Alyson M. *The Cult of True Victimhood: From the War on Welfare to the War on Terror.* Stanford UP, 2006.

Daly, Herman E. "Entropy, Growth, and the Political Economy of Scarcity." *Scarcity and Growth Reconsidered*, edited by V. Kerry Smith, Resources for the Future Press, 1979, pp. 67–95.

Davis, Daniel B. *Contingent Academic Labor: Evaluating Conditions to Improve Student Outcomes.* Stylus Publishing, 2017.

Dawson, Ashley. "Another University is Possible: Academic Labor, the Ideology of Scarcity, and the Fight for Workplace Democracy." *Workplace: A Journal for Academic Labor*, no. 14, 2007, pp. 91–105, https://doi.org/10.14288/workplace.v0i14.182204.

Day, Terence, et al. "The Immediate Impact of COVID-19 on Postsecondary Teaching and Learning." *The Professional Geographer*, vol. 73, no. 1, 2021, 1–13, https://doi.org/10.1080/00330124.2020.1823864.

De Stefano, Valerio. "The Rise of the 'Just-in-Time Workforce': On-Demand Work, Crowdwork, and Labor Protection in the 'Gig Economy.'" *Comparative Labor Law and Policy Journal*, vol. 37, no. 3, 2016, 471–504, https://cllpj.law.illinois.edu/archive/vol_37/download?id=651.

Dobbie, David, and Ian Robinson. "Reorganizing Higher Education in the United States and Canada: The Erosion of Tenure and the Unionization of Contingent Faculty." *Labor Studies Journal*, vol. 33, no. 2, 2008, pp. 117–40, https://doi.org/10.1177%2F0160449X07301241.

Doe, Sue and Mike Palmquist. "An Evolving Discourse: The Shifting Uses of Position Statements on the Contingent Faculty." *ADE Bulletin/ADFL Bulletin*, vol. 153/vol. 42, no. 3, 2013, pp. 23–34, https://www.maps.mla.org/bulletin/pdf/156232.

Doellgast, Virginia, and Chiara Benassi. "Collective Bargaining." *Handbook of Research on Employee Voice*, edited by Adrian Wilkinson et al., Edward Elgar Publishing, 2014, pp. 227–46, https://doi.org/10.4337/9780857939272.00023.

Donhardt, Tracy, and Sarah Layden. "Adjuncts Foster Change: Improving Adjunct Working Conditions by Forming an Associate Faculty Coalition (AFC)." *Contingency,*

Exploitation, and Solidarity: Labor and Action in English Composition, edited by Seth Kahn et al., The WAC Clearinghouse, UP of Colorado, 2017, pp. 183–97, https://doi.org/10.37514/PER-B.2017.0858.2.12.

Donoghue, Frank. *The Last Professors: The Corporate University and the Fate of the Humanities*. Fordham UP, 2018.

Drake, Anna, et al. "Invisible Labor, Visible Change: Non-Tenure-Track Faculty Agency in a Research University." *Review of Higher Education*, vol. 42, no. 4, summer 2019, pp. 1635–64. *Project Muse*, https://doi.org/10.1353/rhe.2019.0078.

Dyke, Nella van. "Crossing Movement Boundaries: Factors That Facilitate Coalition Protest by American College Students, 1930–1990." *Social Problems*, vol. 50, no. 2, May 2003, pp. 226–50, https://doi.org/10.1525/sp.2003.50.2.226.

Eaton, B. Curtis, and Mukesh Eswaran. "Well-Being and Affluence in the Presence of a Veblen Good." *The Economic Journal*, vol. 119, no. 539, Jul. 2009, pp. 1088–104, https://doi.org/10.1111/j.1468-0297.2009.02255.x.

Eaton, Charlie. "Still Public: State Universities and America's New Student-Debt Coalitions." *PS: Political Science and Politics*, vol. 50, no. 2, Apr. 2017, pp. 408–12, https://doi.org/10.1017/S1049096516002912.

Ehrenberg, Ronald G. "American Higher Education in Transition." *Journal of Economic Perspectives*, vol. 26, no. 1, winter 2012, pp. 193–216, https://doi.org/10.1257/jep.26.1.193.

Ehrenreich, Barbara. *Fear of Falling: The Inner Life of the Middle Class*. Twelve, 2020.

Elman, Sandra E. "A Regional Accreditation Perspective on Contingent Faculty Appointments." *New Directions for Higher Education*, vol. 2003, no. 123, fall 2003, pp. 71–78, https://doi.org/10.1002/he.122.

Fay, Daniel L., and Adela Ghadimi. "Collective Bargaining During Times of Crisis: Recommendations from the COVID-19 Pandemic." *Public Administration Review*, vol. 80, no. 5, 2020, pp. 815–19, https://doi.org/10.1111/puar.13233.

Feldman, Daniel C., and William H. Turnley. "Contingent Employment in Academic Careers: Relative Ddeprivation among Adjunct Faculty." *Journal of Vocational Behavior*, vol. 64, no. 2, 2004, pp. 284–307. *ScienceDirect*, https://doi.org/10.1016/j.jvb.2002.11.003.

Fels, Dawn, et al. "Toward an Investigation into the Working Conditions of Non-Tenure Line, Contingent Writing Center Workers." *Forum: Issues about Part-Time and Contingent Faculty*, vol. 20, no. 1, fall 2016, pp. A10-A16, https://library.ncte.org/journals/CCC/issues/v68-1/28758.

Fichtenbaum, Rudy. "Collective Bargaining Results Regarding Contingent Faculty." *Journal of Collective Bargaining in the Academy*, vol. 0, no. 9, 2014, https://thekeep.eiu.edu/jcba/vol0/iss9/24/.

Fleischer, Georgette. "Come Together, Right Now/Over Me, Over You, Over Us." flexible." *International Labor and Working-Class History*, vol. 91, Apr. 2017, pp. 156–63, https://doi.org/10.1017/S0147547916000387.

Frank, Thomas. *Listen, Liberal: Or, What Ever Happened to the Party of the People?* Picador, 2016.

Fricke, Werner. "Thirty Years of Work Life Programmes in Germany." *Concepts and Transformation*, vol. 8, no. 1, Jan. 2003, pp. 43–68, https://doi.org/10.1075/cat.8.1.04fri.

Giroux, Henry A. "Neoliberalism, Corporate Culture, and the Promise of Higher Education: The University as a Democratic Public Sphere." *Harvard Educational Review*, vol. 72, no. 4, winter 2002, pp. 425–64, https://www.hepg.org/her-home/issues/harvard-educational-review-volume-72-issue-4/herarticle/the-university-as-a-democratic-public-sphere_39.

P&C

Godard, John. "Strikes as Collective Voice: A Behavioral Analysis of Strike Activity." *ILR Review*, vol. 46, no. 1, Oct. 1992, pp. 161–75, https://doi.org/10.1177%2F001979399 204600112.

Goldstene, Claire. "The Politics of Contingent Academic Labor." *Thought and Action*, vol. 28, fall 2012, pp. 7–15.

Greene, Jay P., et al.. *Administrative Bloat at American Universities: The Real Reason for High Costs in Higher Education*. Goldwater Institute, 17 Aug. 2010. *Goldwater Institute*, 25 Mar. 2015, http://www.goldwaterinstitute.org/wp-content/uploads/cms_page _media/2015/3/24/Administrative%20Bloat.pdf.

Gulli, Bruno. "Knowledge Production and the Superexploitation of Contingent Academic Labor." *Workplace: A Journal for Academic Labor*, no. 16, 2009, pp. 1–30, https://doi.org/10.14288/workplace.v0i16.182232.

Gutmann, Amy, and Dennis Thompson. *The Spirit of Compromise: Why Governing Demands It and Campaigning Undermines It*. Updated ed., Princeton UP, 2014.

Hedges, Chris. *Death of the Liberal Class*. Vintage Canada, 2011.

Heller, Janet Ruth. "Contingent Faculty and the Evaluation Process." *Forum: Issues about Part-Time and Contingent Faculty*, vol. 16, no. 1, fall 2012, pp. A8–A12, https://library .ncte.org/journals/CCC/issues/v64-1/20862.

Henig, Jeffrey R., and Clarence N. Stone. "Rethinking School Reform: The Distractions of Dogma and the Potential for a New Politics of Progressive Pragmatism." *American Journal of Education*, vol. 114, no. 3, May 2008, pp. 191–218, https://www.journals .uchicago.edu/doi/full/10.1086/529500.

Hoeller, Keith. "The Future of the Contingent Faculty Movement." *Inside Higher Ed*, 13 Nov. 2007, https://www.insidehighered.com/views/2007/11/13/future-contingent -faculty-movement.

Huston, Therese A. "Race and Gender Bias in Higher Education: Could Faculty Course Evaluations Impede Further Progress Toward Parity." *Seattle Journal for Social Justice*, vol. 4, no. 2, 2006, pp. 591–611, https://digitalcommons.law.seattleu.edu/sjsj /vol4/iss2/34/.

Jansen, Stef. "The Streets of Beograd. Urban Space and Protest Identities in Serbia." *Political Geography*, vol. 20, no.1, Jan. 2001, pp. 35–55. *ScienceDirect*, https://doi.org /10.1016/S0962-6298(00)00052-4.

Jarzabkowski, Paula, and Evelyn Fenton. "Strategizing and Organizing in Pluralistic Contexts." *Long Range Planning*, vol. 39, no. 6, Dec. 2006, pp. 631–48. *ScienceDirect*, https://doi.org/10.1016/j.lrp.2006.11.002.

Johnston, Paul. *Success While Others Fail: Social Movement Unionism and the Public Workplace*. ILR Press, 1994.

Jolley, Michael R., et al. "A Critical Challenge: The Engagement and Assessment of Contingent, Part-Time Adjunct Faculty Professors in United States Community Colleges." *Community College Journal of Research and Practice*, vol. 38, no. 2–3, 2014, pp. 218–30, https://doi.org/10.1080/10668926.2014.851969.

Kahn, Seth. "'Never Take More Than You Need': Tenure-Track/Tenured Faculty and Contingent Labor Exploitation." *Forum: Issues about Part-time and Contingent Faculty*, vol. 16, no. 2, spring 2013, A12–A16, https://library.ncte.org/journals/tetyc /issues/v40-3/23066.

Katz, Harry C., et al. "The Revitalization of the CWA: Integrating Collective Bargaining, Political Action, and Organizing." *ILR Review*, vol. 56, no. 4, Jul. 2003, pp. 573–89, https://doi.org/10.1177%2F001979390305600402.

Kehm, Barbara M. "Doctoral Education in Europe and North America: A Comparative Analysis." *Wenner-Gren International Series*, vol. 83, edited by Teichler, Portland Press, 2006, pp. 67–78, https://portlandpress.com/DocumentLibrary/Umbrella /Wenner%20Gren/Vol%2083/Chap07_Wenner_Gren_83.pdf.

Kelly, John. "Conflict: Trends and Forms of Collective Action." *Employee Relations*, vol. 37, no. 6, 2015, pp. 720–32, https://doi.org/10.1108/ER-06-2015-0102.

Kemp, Andrew T. "Collaboration vs. Individualism: What is Better for the Rising Academic?" *The Qualitative Report*, vol. 18, no. 50, 2013, https://doi.org/10.46743 /2160-3715/2013.1429.

Kezar, Adrianna. "Needed Policies, Practices, and Values: Creating a Culture to Support and Professionalize Non-Tenure Track Faculty." *Embracing Non-Tenure Track Faculty: Changing Campuses for the New Faculty*, edited by Adrianna Kezar, Routledge, 2012, pp. 2–27.

——. "Preface." *Embracing Non-Tenure Track Faculty: Changing Campuses for the New Faculty*, edited by Adrianna Kezar, Routledge, 2012, pp. x–xxiv.

Kezar, Adrianna, and Jaime Lester. "Supporting Faculty Grassroots Leadership." *Research in Higher Education*, vol. 50, no. 7, Nov. 2009, pp. 715–40. *Springer Link*, https://doi.org/10.1007/s11162-009-9139-6.

Kezar, Adrianna, and Daniel Maxey. *The Changing Faculty and Student Success: Non-Tenure-Track Faculty Promising Practices*, USC Rossier Pullias Center for Higher Education, 2013, https://pullias.usc.edu/download/changing-faculty-student -success-non-tenure-track-faculty-promising-practices/.

——. "Missing from the Institutional Data Picture: Non-Tenure-Track Faculty." *New Directions for Institutional Research*, vol. 2012, no. 155, fall 2012, pp. 47–65, https:// doi.org/10.1002/ir.20021.

——. "Troubling Ethical Lapses: The Treatment of Contingent Faculty." *Change: The Magazine of Higher Learning*, vol. 46, no. 4, 2014, pp. 34–37, https://doi.org/10.1080/0 0091383.2014.925761.

Kezar, Adrianna, and Cecile Sam. "Governance as a Catalyst for Policy Change: Creating a Contingent Faculty Friendly Academy." *Educational Policy*, vol. 28, no. 3, 2014, pp. 425–62, https://doi.org/10.1177%2F0895904812465112.

——. "Institutionalizing Equitable Policies and Practices for Contingent Faculty." *Journal of Higher Education*, vol. 84, no. 1, 2013, pp. 56–87, https://doi.org/10.1080/00221546 .2013.11777278.

——. "Understanding the New Majority of Non-Tenure-Track Faculty in Higher Education: Demographics, Experiences, and Plans of Action." *ASHE Higher Education Report*, vol. 36, no. 4, 2010, pp. 1–133, https://doi.org/10.1002/aehe.3604.

Kezar, Adrianna, et al. "Challenging Stereotypes That Interfere with Effective Governance." *Thought and Action*, vol. 22, no. 2, fall 2006, pp. 121–34.

Kezar, Adrianna, et al. *The Gig Academy: Mapping Labor in the Neoliberal University*. Johns Hopkins UP, 2019. *Project Muse*, https://doi.org/10.1353/book.68032.

Klare, Karl E. "The Labor-Management Cooperation Debate: A Workplace Democracy Perspective." *Harvard Civil Rights-Civil Liberties Law Review*, vol. 23, no. 1, winter 1988, pp. 39–83, http://hdl.handle.net/2047/d20002626.

Lalicker, William B., and Amy Lynch-Biniek. "Contingency, Solidarity, and Community Buidling: Principles for Converting Contingent to Tenure Track." *Contingency, Exploitation, and Solidarity: Labor and Action in English Composition*, edited by Seth Kahn et al., The WAC Clearinghouse, UP of Colorado, 2017, pp. 91–102, https://doi .org/10.37514/PER-B.2017.0858.2.06.

P&C

Lebowitz, Michael A. "Karl Marx: The Needs of Capital vs. the Needs of Human Beings." *Understanding Capitalism: Critical Analysis from Karl Marx to Amartya Sen*, edited by Douglas Dowd, Pluto Press, 2002, pp. 17–36.

Lee, JongHwa, and Seth Kahn, eds. *Activism and Rhetoric: Theories and Contexts for Political Engagement*. 2nd ed., Routledge, 2019, https://doi.org/10.4324/9781315144535.

Levin, John S., and Genevieve G. Shaker. "The Hybrid and Dualistic Identity of Full-Time Non-Tenure-Track Faculty." *American Behavioral Scientist*, vol. 55, no. 11, 2011, pp. 1461–84, https://doi.org/10.1177%2F0002764211409382.

Levkoe, Charles Z. "Strategies for Forging and Sustaining Social Movement Networks: A Case Study of Provincial Food Networking Organizations in Canada." *Geoforum*, vol. 58, Jan. 2015, pp. 174–83. *ScienceDirect*, https://doi.org/10.1016/j.geoforum.2014.11.013.

Lind, Carol, and Joan Mullin. "Silent Subversion, Quiet Competence, and Patient Persistence." *Contingency, Exploitation, and Solidarity: Labor and Action in English Composition*, edited by Seth Kahn et al., The WAC Clearinghouse, UP of Colorado, 2017, pp. 13–26, https://doi.org/10.37514/PER-B.2017.0858.2.01.

Lobel, Orly. "The Gig Economy and the Future of Employment and Labor Law." *University of San Francisco Law Review*, vol. 51, no. 1, 2018.

Lowen, Rebecca S. *Creating the Cold War University: The Transformation of Stanford*. U of California P, 1997.

Macy, Michael, and Andreas Flache. "Social Dynamics from the Bottom Up: Agent-Based Models of Social Interaction." *The Oxford Handbook of Analytical Sociology*, edited by Peter Bearman and Peter Hedström, Oxford UP, 2011, pp. 245–68, https://doi.org/10.1093/oxfordhb/9780199215362.013.11.

Maitland, Christine, and Gary Rhoades. "Bargaining for Contingent Faculty." *The NEA 2005 Almanac of Higher Education*, National Education Association, 2005, pp. 75–83.

Markowitz, Linda. *Worker Activism after Successful Union Organizing*. Routledge, 2015, https://doi.org/10.4324/9781315698076.

Marshall, Eric. "Victims of Circumstance: Academic Freedom in a Contingent Academy." *Academe*, vol. 89, no. 3, May-June 2003, pp. 45–49. *JSTOR*, https://doi.org/10.2307/40252469.

Maxey, Daniel, and Adrianna Kezar. "Revealing Opportunities and Obstacles for Changing Non-Tenure-Track Faculty Practices: An Examination of Stakeholders' Awareness of Institutional Contradictions." *The Journal of Higher Education*, vol. 86, no. 4, 2015, pp. 564–94, https://doi.org/10.1080/00221546.2015.11777375.

Mayer, Robert. "Robert Dahl and the Right to Workplace Democracy." *The Review of Politics*, vol. 63, no. 2, spring 2001, pp. 221–47, https://doi.org/10.1017/S0034670500031156.

Mbuva, James M. "Exploration of the Promoting of the Non-Tenure Track Position as a Means of Enhancing Teaching and Professional Effectiveness in Higher Education: A Reflective Case Analysis of Non-Tenure Track Position Model in a Private University." *Journal of Higher Education Theory and Practice*, vol. 19, no. 3, 2019, https://doi.org/10.33423/jhetp.v19i3.2118.

McBeth, Mark, and Tim McCormack. "An Apologia and a Way Forward: In Defense of the Lecturer Line in Writing Programs." *Contingency, Exploitation, and Solidarity: Labor and Action in English Composition*, edited by Seth Kahn et al., The WAC Clearinghouse, UP of Colorado, 2017, pp. 41–55, https://doi.org/10.37514/PER-B.2017.0858.2.03.

McGrew, Heidi, and Joe Untener. "A Primer on Improving Contingent Faculty Conditions." *Academe*, vol. 96, no. 4, 2010, https://www.aaup.org/article/primer-improving-contingent-faculty-conditions.

McNamee, Stephen J., and Robert K. Miller. *The Meritocracy Myth*. Rowman and Littlefield, 2009.

Melucci, Alberto. "A Strange Kind of Newness: What's 'New' in New Social Movements?" *New Social Movements: From Ideology to Identity*, edited by Enrique Laraña et al., Temple UP, 1994, pp. 101–30. *JSTOR*, http://www.jstor.org/stable/j.ctt14bst9g.7.

Merritt, Deborah J. "Bias, the brain, and student evaluations of teaching." *St. John's Law Review*, vol. 82, no. 1, winter 2008, pp. 235–87, https://scholarship.law.stjohns.edu/lawreview/vol82/iss1/6/.

Monks, James. "Who Are the Part-Time Faculty?" *Academe*, vol. 95, no. 4, July-Aug. 2009, https://www.aaup.org/article/who-are-part-time-faculty.

Morio, Hiroaki, and Christopher Buchholz. "How Anonymous Are You Online? Examining Online Social Behaviors from a Cross-Cultural Perspective." *AI and Society*, vol. 23, no. 2, Mar. 2009, pp. 297–307. *SpringerLink*, https://doi.org/10.1007/s00146-007-0143-0.

Morris, Libby V. "Faculty Redefined." *Innovative Higher Education*, vol. 34, no.3, Aug. 2009, pp. 131–32. *Springer Link*, https://doi.org/10.1007/s10755-009-9115-2.

Nealon, Jeffrey. *Post-Postmodernism: Or, the Cultural Logic of Just-in-Time Capitalism*. Stanford UP, 2012.

Nelson, Cary, ed. *Will Teach for Food*. U Minnesota P, 1997.

Newfield, Christopher. *The Great Mistake: How We Wrecked Public Universities and How We Can Fix Them*. Johns Hopkins UP, 2018.

Nisbet, Robert A. *The Degradation of the Academic Dogma*. Routledge, 1997, https://doi.org/10.4324/9781351304962.

Noll, Roger G., and William P. Rogerson. "The Economics of University Indirect Cost Reimbursement in Federal Research Grants." *SSRN*, 1998, https://papers.ssrn.com/sol3/papers.cfm?abstract_id=78786. Working paper.

Norgaard, Rolf. "The Uncertain Future of Past Success: Memory, Narrative, and the Dynamics of Institutional Change." *Contingency, Exploitation, and Solidarity: Labor and Action in English Composition*, edited by Seth Kahn et al., The WAC Clearinghouse, UP of Colorado, 2017, pp. 133–49, https://doi.org/0.37514/PER-B.2017.0858.2.09.

Oppenheim, Lisa. "Women's Ways of Organizing: A Conversation with AFSCME Organizers Kris Rondeau and Gladys McKenzie." *Labor Research Review*, vol. 1, no. 18, 1991, pp. 45–59, https://hdl.handle.net/1813/102579.

Ostrander, Jason A., et al. "Collective Power to Create Political Change: Increasing the Political Efficacy and Engagement of Social Workers." *Journal of Policy Practice*, vol. 16, no. 3, 2017, pp. 261–75, https://doi.org/10.1080/15588742.2016.1266296.

Palmquist, Mike et al. "Statement on the Status and Working Conditions of Contingent Faculty." *College English*, Mar. 2011, vol. 73, no. 4, pp. 356–59, https://library.ncte.org/journals/ce/issues/v73-4/13513.

Pausch, Markus. "Workplace Democracy: From a Democratic Ideal to a Managerial Tool and Back." *The Innovation Journal*, vol. 19, no. 1, 2014, https://innovation.cc/scholarly-style/2014_19_1_3_pausch_workplace-democracy.pdf.

Pham, Nhung, and Valerie Osland Paton. "Regional Accreditation Standards and Contingent and Part-Time Faculty." New Directions for Institutional Research vol. 2017, no. 176, winter 2017, pp. 41–54, https://doi.org/10.1002/ir.20243.

Pratt, Linda Ray. "Disposable Faculty: Part-Time Exploitation as Management Strategy." *Will Teach for Food*, edited by Cary Nelson, U Minnesota P, 1997, pp. 264–77.

Rhoades, Gary. "Bargaining Quality in Part-Time Faculty Working Conditions: Beyond Just-in-Time Employment and Just-at-Will Non-Renewal." *Journal of Collective Bargaining in the Academy*, vol. 4, no. 1, 2013, https://thekeep.eiu.edu/jcba/vol4/iss1/4/.

——. "Creative Leveraging in Contingent Faculty Organizing." *Journal of Labor and Society*, vol. 18, no. 3, Sep. 2015, pp. 435–45, https://doi.org/10.1111/wusa.12191.

Rhoades, Gary, and Christine Maitland. "Bargaining for Full-Time, Non-Tenure Track Faculty: Best Practices." *The NEA 2008 Almanac of Higher Education*, National Education Association, 2008, pp. 67–73.

Robert, Henry Martyn. *Robert's Rules of Order Revised for Deliberative Assemblies*. Scott, Foresman and Company, 1915.

Ross, Andrew. Nice Work If You Can Get It: Life and Labor in Precarious Times. New York UP, 2009.

Sacks, Peter. *Generation X Goes to College. An Eye-Opening Account of Teaching in Postmodern America*. Open Court, 1996.

Samuels, Bob. "Contingent Faculty and Academic Freedom in the Age of Trump: Organizing the Disenfranchised Is the Key to Success." *Forum: Issues about Part-Time and Contingent Faculty*, vol. 21, no. 2, spring 2018, A21-A24, https://library.ncte.org/journals/tetyc/issues/v45-4/29665.

——. "Corporatizing the Instructorate: Ceding Authority to the Administrative Class." *Forum: Newsletter for Issues about Part-Time and Contingent Faculty*, vol. 13, no. 1, fall 2009, pp. A8-A10, https://library.ncte.org/journals/CCC/issues/v61-1/8307.

——. "(Liberal) Narcissism." *Routledge Handbook of Psychoanalytic Political Theory*, edited by Yannis Stavrakakis, Routledge, 2020, pp. 151–61.

Samuels, Robert. *Educating Inequality: Beyond the Political Myths of Higher Education and the Job Market*. Routledge, 2018, https://doi.org/10.4324/9781315111582.

——. *The Politics of Writing Studies: Reinventing Our Universities from Below*. Utah State UP, 2017. JSTOR, https://doi.org/10.2307/j.ctt1v2xts5.

——. *Why Public Higher Education Should Be Free: How to Decrease Cost and Increase Quality at American Universities*. Rutgers UP, 2013. JSTOR, https://www.jstor.org/stable/j.ctt5hjcow.

Scherr, Frederick C., and Susan S. Scherr. "Bias in Student Evaluations of Teacher Effectiveness." *Journal of Education for Business*, vol. 65, no. 8, May 1990, pp. 356–58.

Schmidt, Jeff. *Disciplined Minds: A Critical Look at Salaried Professionals and the Soul-Battering System That Shapes Their Lives*. Rowman and Littlefield, 2000.

Schneirov, Richard. "Contingent Faculty: A New Social Movement Takes Shape." *Journal of Labor and Society*, vol. 6, no. 4, Mar. 2003, pp. 38–48, https://doi.org/10.1111/j.1743-4580.2003.00038.x.

Schwartz, Joseph M. "Resisting the Exploitation of Contingent Faculty Labor in the Neoliberal University: The Challenge of Building Solidarity between Tenured and Non-Tenured Faculty." *New Political Science*, vol. 36, no. 4, 2014, pp. 504–22, https://doi.org/10.1080/07393148.2014.954803.

Semuels, Alana. "What Happens When Gig Economy Workers Become Employees?" *The Atlantic*, 14 Sept. 2018, https://www.theatlantic.com/technology/archive/2018/09/gig-economy-independent-contractors/570307/.

Shillington, Audrey Mengwasser, et al. "COVID-19 and Long-Term Impacts on Tenure-Line Careers." *Journal of the Society for Social Work and Research*, vol. 11, no. 4, 2020, pp. 499–507, https://doi.org/10.1086/712579.

Slaughter, Sheila, and Gary Rhoades. *Academic Capitalism and the New Economy: Markets, State, and Higher Education.* Johns Hopkins UP, 2004.

Sloterdijk, Peter. *Critique of Cynical Reason.* Translated by Michael Eldred, Verso Press, 1988.

Spaniel, Suzann H., and Joyce A. Scott. "Community College Adjunct Faculty Inclusion: Variations by Institution Type." *Research in Higher Education Journal*, vol. 21, Aug. 2013, https://www.aabri.com/manuscripts/131569.pdf.

Stephan, Paula. "How to Exploit Postdocs." *BioScience*, vol. 63, no. 4, Apr. 2013, pp. 245–46, https://doi.org/10.1525/bio.2013.63.4.2.

Street, Steve, et al. *Who is Professor "Staff," and How Can This Person Teach So Many Classes?* Campaign for the Future of Higher Education, 2012. https://www.futureofhighered.org/sites/main/files/file-attachments/profstafffinal1.pdf?1483569612.

Tam, Teresa, and Daniel Jacoby. "What We Can't Say about Contingent Faculty." *Academe*, vol. 95, no. 3, 2009, https://www.aaup.org/issue/may-june-2009.

Thompson, Karen. "Alchemy in the Academy: Moving Part-Time Faculty from Piecework to Parity." *Will Teach for Food*, edited by Cary Nelson, U Minnesota P, 1997, pp. 278–90.

——. "Contingent Faculty and Student Learning: Welcome to the Strativersity." *New Directions for Higher Education*, vol. 2003, no. 123, fall 2003, pp. 41–47, https://doi.org/10.1002/he.119.

Tingle, Nick. "UC-AFT Lecturers Engage in Systematic Labor Unrest!" *Workplace: The Journal for Academic Labor*, vol. 5, no. 1, Oct. 2002, https://louisville.edu/journal/workplace/issue5p1/tinglereportage.html.

Toren, Nina. "Deprofessionalization and Its Sources: A Preliminary Analysis." *Work and Occupations*, vol. 2, no. 4, 1975, pp. 323–37, https://doi.org/10.1177%2F0730888475002000402.

Trout, Paul. "Deconstructing an Evaluation Form." *The Montana Professor*, vol. 8, no. 3, fall 1998, https://mtprof.msun.edu/Fall1998/TroutArt.html.

Turner, Lowell, and Richard W. Hurd. "Building Social Movement Unionism: The Transformation of the American Labor Movement." *Rekindling the Movement: Labor's Quest for Relevance in the Twenty-First Century*, edited by Lowell Turner et al., ILR Press, 2001, pp. 9–26.

Uetricht, Micah. *Strike for America: Chicago Teachers Against Austerity.* Verso, 2014.

Vardi, Moshe Y. "Will MOOCs Destroy Academia?" *Communications of the ACM*, vol. 55, no. 11, Nov. 2012, p. 5, https://doi.org/10.1145/2366316.2366317.

Waltman, Jean, et al. "Factors Contributing to Job Satisfaction and Dissatisfaction among Non-Tenure-Track Faculty." *The Journal of Higher Education*, vol. 83, no. 3, 2012, pp. 411–34, https://doi.org/10.1080/00221546.2012.11777250.

Washburn, Jennifer. *University, Inc.: The Corporate Corruption of Higher Education.* Basic Books, 2005.

White, Judith S. "Excluded by Choice? Contingent Faculty and the Leadership Core." *On Campus with Women*, vol. 37, no. 3, 2009, p. 11.

Whittier, Nancy. "Identity Politics, Consciousness-Raising, and Visibility Politics." *The Oxford Handbook of U.S. Women's Social Movement Activism*, edited by Holly J. McCammon et al., Oxford UP, 2017, pp. 376–97, https://doi.org/10.1093/oxfordhb/9780190204204.013.20.

P&C

Yates, Charlotte AB. "Understanding Caring, Organizing Women: How Framing a Problem Shapes Union Strategy." *Transfer: European Review of Labour and Research*, vol. 16, no. 3, Aug. 2010, pp. 399–410, https://doi.org/10.1177%2F1024258910373870.

Zinn, Howard. *A People's History of the United States 1492-Present*. 3rd ed., Routledge, 2015.

Žižek, Slavoj, and Ernesto Laclau. London: Verso, 1989.

About the Author

Robert Samuels teaches writing at the University of California Santa Barbara. He is the author of 18 books, including *Teaching Writing, Rhetoric, and Reason at the Globalizing University* and *The Politics of Writing Studies.* He is the former president of UC-AFT, a union representing contingent faculty in the University of California system.